27

5.99

Self Hypnosis

REVISED EDITION

Easy Ways
to **Hypnotize**
Your **Problems** Away

DR. BRUCE GOLDBERG

DEDICATION

This book is dedicated to the thousands of my patients who have been kind enough to use self-hypnosis for a myriad of improvements, without whom this book would not have been possible. I also dedicate this book to the Universe, whose many wonders never cease to both amaze and instruct me in the art and science of self-hypnosis.

ACKNOWLEDGMENTS

I would like to thank Michael Lewis, Acquisitions Editor at New Page Books, for his interest and assistance in bringing this book to the public. In addition, my heartfelt gratitude goes out to the editorial staff at Innovation Publication Services. Without their experience and detailed supervision, this book's final form would be quite different. Finally, I cannot express enough appreciation to my typist, Marianne Colasanti, for her tireless efforts and spiritual support.

NOTE TO READER

This book is the result of the professional experiences accumulated by the author since 1974, working individually with more than 14,000 patients. The material included herein is intended to complement, not replace, the advice of your own physician, psychotherapist, or other healthcare professional, whom you should always consult about your circumstances before starting or stopping any medication or any other course of treatment, exercise regimen, or diet. At times, the masculine pronoun has been used as a convenience. It is intended to indicate both male and female genders where this is applicable. All names and identifying references, except those of celebrities, have been altered to protect the privacy of my patients. All other facts are accurate and have not been altered.

CONTENTS

How to Use
This Book

This book contains dozens of exercises specifically designed to train you to experience self-hypnosis. It doesn't matter what your background is.

You can accept or reject any of the principles and concepts presented here. Empowerment is vital. I stress this in my Los Angeles hypnotherapy practice and in my personal life as well. If you become rigid and stuck in your views, you become trapped by your beliefs. You are no longer empowered because you are no longer free.

Always use your judgment and free will in trying these exercises. Use the ones you feel comfortable with and ignore the others. These exercises are all perfectly safe and have been tested for more than 25 years. You may create your own exercises from these models.

Read each exercise thoroughly to become familiar with it. Use the relaxation techniques given, or your own. You may practice alone or with others. I strongly suggest that you make tapes of these exercises. Read the scripts slowly and leave enough space on your tape to experience each part of the procedure.

Practice once or twice a day, in 15- to 20-minute sessions. In general, it is considered most effective to practice in the morning, as it may provide a relaxing start for the entire day. The more specific and realistic your schedule, the better the chances that you will succeed.

You should choose a part of your day when you are at your best. If you wait to practice until long after you get home from a hard day at work, you

11

might only practice going to sleep. Self-hypnosis is most effective if practiced when you are reasonably alert. Begin by picking a good time to practice.

If you wake up alert and rested first thing in the morning, practice then, before getting out of bed. Take into account whether or not you will be disturbed by a spouse, lover, kids, pets, and so forth. Choose a time when you are not likely to be interrupted. Other popular times are before lunch or dinner.

Four components of successful self-hypnosis are:

- ◆ A quiet environment.
- ◆ A mental device.
- ◆ A passive attitude.
- ◆ A comfortable position.

When you enter into a self-hypnotic trance, you will observe the following:

- ◆ A positive mood (tranquility, peace of mind).
- ◆ An experience of unity or oneness with the environment.
- ◆ An inability to describe the experience in words.
- ◆ An alteration in time/space relationships.
- ◆ An enhanced sense of reality and meaning.

If you experience difficulty with an exercise, do not become frustrated. Some techniques are quite advanced, and you may not be ready for all of them. Return to the ones you could not successfully work with at another time.

Practice these trance states when you have time and are relaxed. Be patient. It takes time to master trance states and to become accustomed to this new and wonderful world. No one way is the right way to experience a trance. Your body may feel light, or it may feel heavy; you may feel as if you are dreaming; your eyelids may flutter; or your body can become cooler or warmer. All these possible responses are perfectly safe.

Because at first you will be unfamiliar with the techniques, your initial practice sessions should run as long as you need. As you become more proficient, you will be able to shorten these sessions. Some days nothing may seem to work. Try not to become discouraged. Remember that other days will be more fruitful. Always work at your own pace and with an open mind.

CHAPTER 1

WHAT IS
HYPNOSIS?

Hypnosis is not a new discipline, and its use can be traced back to ancient Egypt. Actually, hypnosis is present in our lives today in the form of advertising, teaching, sales, healthcare, and religion.

Hypnosis is a fascinating subject that has been unjustly surrounded by myths and distortions, such as connotations of magic, the supernatural, and the occult. Many movies and novels have contributed to these misconceptions. Since World War II, experimentation and practice have led to rapid advances in our knowledge and techniques—spurred on by its widespread acceptance in 1958 by the American Medical Association.

Hypnosis is being taught to doctors, police officers, lawyers, clergymen, salesmen, athletes, executives, students, and many others who have found it beneficial to their professions. All hypnosis is really self-hypnosis—a state that the subject produces himself with the hypnotist serving only as the guide or the teacher. Anyone who is willing to apply himself/herself can learn this technique.

Everyone can be hypnotized to some extent. People will, however, vary as to the depth acquired and the length of time required for conditioning. All one needs to experience self-hypnosis is a desire and the application of simple techniques.

Hypnosis is not a medicine or cure. It is a powerful tool that may be used in therapy to assist people in such goals as developing self-confidence, controlling habits, overcoming shyness, relieving insomnia, developing hidden talents, improving memory and concentration, and putting more order into life.

Hypnosis is a natural state of focused concentration and relaxation. Let me further clarify this level of consciousness by asserting that hypnosis is a way of relaxing and setting aside the conscious mind (willpower), while at the same time activating the subconscious mind. Suggestions can then be made directly to the subconscious, enabling the individual to act on these suggestions with greater ease and efficiency.

Hypnosis can be described by the following formula:

misdirected attention + belief + expectation = hypnosis

Until relatively recently, hypnosis has been viewed as either a mysterious or dangerous, artificially induced technique. Nothing could be further from the truth. There is nothing magical or mystical about hypnosis. It is a state of consciousness that is entered naturally, but is not usually called hypnosis or trance. It is simply labeled a daydream.

This ancient art known as hypnosis has been used to promote healing for more than 50,000 years! More than 2,500 hours each year of your life are spent in natural hypnosis. Each day, four hours of this total constitutes daydreams, and night dreams (REM cycle) account for three additional hours.

For a 40-year-old individual, the average total number of hours spent in natural hypnosis throughout his or her life is about 100,000. That is equivalent to doing some menial task that you have completed hundreds of times for eight uninterrupted hours a day, five days a week, 50 weeks per year for 50 years. Remember, this hypothetical reader is only 40 years old!

We concentrate using only our conscious mind (willpower) with an efficiency I would estimate at between 10 percent and 25 percent. The subconscious mind's concentration efficiency rate ranges from 50 percent to

100 percent. Using a natural self-hypnosis exercise enables us to improve our brainpower from 200 percent to 1,000 percent!

The five main characteristics of hypnosis are:

1. Relaxation.
2. Focused concentration.
3. Immobility.
4. Hyperawareness of the five senses.
5. Rapid eye movements.

The term *heterohypnosis* is used to describe the induction of a subject into a hypnotic trance by another person (the hypnotist). If an individual does this to himself, it is referred to as self-hypnosis, or *autohypnosis*. Because all hypnosis is self-hypnosis, it is the subject who describes when to accept this hypnotic state. The gift of hypnosis always lies with the subject, not the hypnotist. The hypnotist may set the stage and create an appropriate environment, but he cannot force the hypnotic state on the subject.

The subconscious mind is a computer it and stores everything we observe with our five senses. This explains how we can significantly increase our brainpower through the use of self-hypnosis, because hypnosis taps in to the subconscious. Remember, hypnosis is neither dangerous nor a form of mind control.

People who are creative, freely express their emotions, are intelligent, and can visualize make the best hypnotic subjects. The poorest candidates are individuals who possess poor visual abilities, are inhibited, have short attention spans, are overly critical, have low levels of intelligence, and are too logical. Even these people, however, can be trained with self-hypnosis.

Think of yourself driving to and from work every day. Notice how you are unaware of the various exits on the highway. Perhaps your mind is focused on a dinner date, business problem, or family matter. This daydream level is a natural form of self-hypnosis, as is the half-awake state you slip into just before falling asleep. These states are sometimes called *altered states of consciousness* (ASC). That is an inaccurate term, because these are, in fact, natural states of consciousness.

The subconscious is childlike, habitual, and simplistic in its reactions, responding to an incident with little regard for logic. Compare this with the purely logical and analytical, conscious mind proper, or willpower. Because the two parts of the mind are not directly connected, it is difficult to change subconscious patterns through the conscious mind or willpower alone. Various forms of psychotherapy attempt to bridge the gap between the conscious and subconscious minds. Hypnotherapy has proved to be much more effective in helping people to make desired changes because it bypasses the conscious mind and goes directly to the subconscious, where behavior patterns are stored.

It is the subconscious mind that primarily influences behavior. It acts like a computer program. Hypnosis reprograms the subconscious. It is far easier to bring changes from the subconscious into conscious behavior than it is to make conscious decisions about desired behavior and have those behaviors manifest from the subconscious. Using hypnosis, you can reprogram your subconscious to make the changes you desire for personal growth and transformation. By tapping into your subconscious, you are using a far greater portion of your mind automatically.

This mind is like a recording device, and our thoughts are simply the recordings we play. If we program ourselves to be average, using less than 1 percent of our brains, that will be our reality. Using the simple act of self-hypnosis, however, we can bring to fruition a very powerful reprogramming and change our behavior and attitudes.

In hypnosis, we alter our internal world by using our imagination. When you change how you think, visualize, and imagine things to be, your feelings and behavior will begin to change to manifest these goals. Hypnosis allows us to present an ideal, such as increased brainpower, to our subconscious, which then transforms this suggestion into a reality. The changes just seem to occur on their own.

The subconscious mind sorts all memories; anything and everything we have experienced through all our senses are located in an organized fashion. As we learn to relax during stress, using the actual stressors as catalysts, the door of the subconscious mind opens, and we are free to work with this powerful part of the mind.

Instead of considering hypnosis an altered state of consciousness, I prefer to view it as a *reversed* state of consciousness. In our normal waking state, the conscious mind is dominant and the subconscious is secondary. When you are functioning in a conscious, or awake, state you are usually unaware of the presence of the underlying subconscious. In a hypnotic state, you are functioning primarily from your subconscious, while your conscious mind is passive. The conscious mind is that state from which we function during normal waking life.

When people are conversing with one another, working out a mathematical problem, or evaluating a purchase, they are working from their conscious minds. When people are engrossed in a novel, daydreaming about a recent event, practicing relaxation techniques, or on the verge of falling asleep, they are functioning from their subconscious. It is important to understand that suggestions given to the subconscious are perceived as already realized by the conscious.

Hypnosis can initiate changes and promote growth in the following areas of your life:

1. Increased relaxation and the elimination of tension.
2. Increased and focused concentration.
3. Improved memory (*hypermnesia*).
4. Improved reflexes.
5. Increased self-confidence.
6. More effective pain control.
7. Improved sex life.
8. Increased organization and efficiency.
9. Increased motivation.
10. Improved interpersonal relationships.
11. Slower aging process.
12. An enhanced career path.
13. Reduced levels of anxiety and depression.
14. Overcoming bereavement.

15. Elimination of headaches, including migraine headaches.
16. Elimination of allergies and skin disorders.
17. Strengthened immune system to resist any disease.
18. Elimination of habits, phobias, and other negative tendencies (self-defeating sequences).
19. Improved decisiveness.
20. Improved quality of people and circumstances that you attract into your life.
21. Increased ability to earn and hold onto money.
22. Elimination or reduction of obsessive-compulsive behavior.
23. Elimination of insomnia.
24. Improved overall quality of life.
25. Improved psychic awareness.
26. Establishment and maintenance of harmony of body, mind, and spirit.

A hypnotic suggestion is effective only when it is accompanied by a misdirection of attention, or a diversion. A reduction in the critical function of the conscious mind proper then ensues, and this allows the suggestion (an uncritical acceptance of an idea) to take hold in the individual's subconscious. When one suggestion after another is accepted, more difficult ones are accepted. This is called *abstract conditioning* and, in part, helps to explain the role that suggestibility plays in the production of hypnotic phenomena. Hypnotic susceptibility depends on motivation. It is a condition of emotional readiness during which perceptual alterations can be induced.

A Self-Hypnosis Exercise

(This exercise can be found on track 1 of the CD in the back of this book.)

One of the simplest methods of experiencing self-hypnosis is through systematically tensing and relaxing various muscles of your body to both differentiate and control these responses. As you practice this exercise, be sure to keep your lips slightly parted. You should also maintain deep, smooth, and rhythmic breathing. Support your head so that it does not rock back and forth.

Take a deep breath and hold it for a count of eight. Now let it out slowly. Repeat this once again and allow your eyes to close. Focus your thoughts on your right hand and make a fist, squeezing it tightly. Hold this sensation for five seconds. Now let go and allow your fingers spread outward, letting out all the tension. As you unclench your fist, you will notice tingling sensations in your hand. This is the tension being released from the muscle. Note the difference between how your right hand felt when you were tensing it and how it feels now. Repeat this procedure with your left hand.

Now lift your eyebrows as high as you can and hold for five seconds. Let go and relax. Next, bring the eyebrows together and, again, hold for five seconds. Let go.

Close your eyes tightly and, simultaneously, wrinkle your nose for five seconds. Let go. Clench your teeth together for five seconds, and then let go.

Push your chin down toward your chest while pulling your head back in the opposite direction. Hold for five seconds, and then let go. Bring your shoulder blades together, bringing them back as if to touch them. Hold for five seconds, and then let go.

Arch your lower back away from the back of the chair. Hold for five seconds, and then let go. Tense your bicep muscles in your right arm and hold for five seconds. Let go. Repeat this procedure with the biceps in your left arm. Now tense all the muscles in both arms. Hold for five seconds, and then let go.

Tense your thigh muscles by trying to push your knees together at the same time. Hold for five seconds, and then let go. Tense your right calf muscle and hold for five seconds. Let go. Repeat this process with your left calf.

Curl your toes as if you were making a fist and hold for five seconds. Let go. Maintain relaxation in your calves and thighs while you are working with your feet.

Now allow the warm, heavy, relaxing feelings you have created to flow throughout your body, permeating deep into each muscle fiber. Check for any areas of tension in your body. Start at your toes, while maintaining a deep relaxation, and run a check up your body through all the muscles with which you have worked. Check some muscles that have not been talked about; if you find them tense, try this exercise on that muscle group.

As you become more proficient with this exercise, increase the tension time from five to 10 seconds.

In modern-day hypnotherapy, we observe that if the muscular tension constituting anxiety can be removed by relaxation, functioning will be improved. Tension manifests itself in many ways, including: overeating, chain smoking, impotency, premature ejaculation, inability to achieve orgasm, phobias, compulsions, depression, and myriad psychosomatic complaints (such as ulcers, asthma, hypertension, and certain types of cardiac disorders). The severity of these ailments is directly proportional to the amount of anxiety present—in a day filled with more exasperation than typical, the cigarette smoker will smoke more, the phobic will be more fearful, the ulcer patient will experience more pain, and so on.

Three alternatives are available to a person when faced with an anxiety-arousing situation: (1) avoid the situation; (2) change the situation; or (3) change the reaction to the situation.

The most effective way to change your feelings about a given situation is to respond with a different sensory reaction to the particular stimulus that previously produced the anxiety. For example, the potential anxiety-provoking stimulus of a tyrannical boss, misbehaving child, or nagging spouse can be neutralized by creating an imagery that produces relaxation. Any pleasant scene that can be constructed in the mind's eye produces relaxation.

A form of counterconditioning is established now by pairing an anxiety-provoking stimulus with one eliciting an incompatible response, such as relaxation. The most vivid imagination uses all the sensory modalities and requires deep concentration. The most effective means to obtain control over sensory recall is the induction procedure used in hypnosis. Once a suitable relaxing scene and the most effective techniques of relaxation and hypnosis are mastered, the scene can be turned on and off at will.

The Hypnotic Trance

The word *trance* is popularly thought of as describing an unusual state of mind. Trance is usually understood to be an *altered* state of consciousness, and not the normal one. And the word *trance* is often associated with the word *hypnosis*. Traditionally, the term *trance* was used to describe certain states that yogis, spiritualist mediums, or channelers might enter to perform their particularly extraordinary behaviors.

Both words have negative connotations in the sense that they imply a loss of conscious, individual will. The negative connotations may lead most people to be unaware of the extent to which trance exists in all areas of life. Even more important, trance techniques can be, and are, used in advertising and social control. Making you aware of these techniques is one main purpose of this book.

A trance is experienced in daydreaming, dancing, listening to music, reading a book, or watching television, and it can be induced through rhythmic and repetitive movement, such as dancing, running, and breathing exercises as well as through chanting, meditation, prayer, and group rituals. In addition, a trance can be induced by focusing attention on an image, an idea, or the sound of someone's voice as well as through relaxation, massage, and warm baths. And it can be induced through drugs such as alcohol, hallucinogens, or tranquilizers.

To me, trance is a relatively common mental state, and there appears to be a continuum from what may be called *normal thinking* to intense, deep, and extraordinary trance states. Prayer, meditation, and chanting will all induce trance. When taken to extremes in the hands of experts, the effect of trance can produce many magical effects, including healing of the body, discovering hidden knowledge, gaining knowledge of the future, and influencing social beliefs. In addition, religious trance can produce an easy tolerance and acceptance of many of life's inevitable disappointments.

The Experience of Hypnosis

During a hypnotherapy session you know you may be open to suggestion. Rather than losing control, a comprehensive series of sessions can help a person to gain control. If during the initial consultation I am not convinced of my new patient's firm commitment to a proclaimed goal, I will not continue with the person. In spite of the increased suggestibility inherent with hypnosis, genuine motivation is necessary for a person to achieve meaningful results in therapy. Patients become more motivated to reach their goals if significant underlying resistance issues get properly addressed and there is some degree of rapport with the therapist.

Many persons who have not previously experienced a formal hypnotic induction expect the experience of the state of hypnosis to be far different, and often more extreme, than what it is. Even after attempts prior to the induction to alleviate such misconceptions, a classic response after a first hypnosis is, "I know I wasn't hypnotized. I heard every word you said." Ironically, the same person, when asked what this "non-hypnosis" experience was like, may give a dramatic response, such as, "Well, I haven't relaxed so much in 20 years." (The initial subjective experience of the state is often disappointing to some extent, but the results can nevertheless be profound.) Some will doubt in early sessions whether they went into hypnosis at all. Others who achieve significant depth may believe only light hypnosis was achieved. With continuing experience, people tend to go deeper and also begin to recognize the signs that, for them, are associated with hypnosis.

Rather than losing consciousness during hypnosis, there is typically heightened consciousness. Awareness is much greater than normal, which is related to the increased focus previously described.

There are many therapy or healing practices that include forms of hypnosis. Biofeedback techniques, for instance, are used in conjunction with hypnosis. Christian Scientists use hypnotic methods for pain control. Guided imagery, guided fantasy, visualization, selective awareness, autogenic training, progressive relaxation, and relaxology are examples of hypnotic methods. Sometimes the practitioner (teacher, nurse, psychotherapist, and so on) using such methods will not associate the methods with hypnosis. If these methods are recognized as hypnotic, and this is communicated to the client, time needs to be taken to alleviate possible misconceptions.

Stage Hypnosis

Misconceptions about hypnosis are still fairly prevalent, but are gradually diminishing with time. The fear of loss of control is a result, in part, of stage hypnosis demonstrations. Volunteers may seem to be "under the spell" of the stage hypnotist. Some develop the notion that the participants will do whatever the hypnotist suggests. Actually, some operators have been known to survey the audience and express disappointment if, say, five volunteers are needed and there are only 60 people in the audience because most people will not respond well to stage hypnosis (and those who do, will do so only under the right circumstances).

Stage hypnosis is a chance for a person with some extrovert tendencies to perform, have fun, and be a star. It is no coincidence that the longest running stage hypnosis show in history, with Pat Collins, was taped in Hollywood. A large percentage of volunteers for her show were striving to become actors and actresses. Volunteers of any stage show know they will be expected to do silly things in front of an audience, and find that appealing. The ones who show timid or self-conscious responses are asked early on to go back to the audience. The participants who are receptive to hypnosis will have, to some extent, a loss of inhibition. However, the volunteer would not do anything against his or her moral beliefs. For example, if handed an imaginary glass of champagne, a nondrinker will refuse to pretend to drink. Also, some otherwise responsive

person will back off to a specific suggestion (for example, to sing) because of a lack of self-confidence in that area. Even during stage hypnosis, individuals retain control in areas of principle or in which there is a
major subconscious resistance.

Music

Music exerts quite an effect upon our behavior. Fast beats make us
aroused and alert. Slow, quiet music calms and relaxes us. High-pitched
music comes across as playful and happy, while low-pitched music is associated with serious or sad moods.

Nature sounds can also be very soothing, renewing, and relaxing.
Sounds emanating from the ocean, the chirping of birds, rain, the wind
rustling through trees, the chatter of squirrels, and so on, have a definite
effect upon us.

Aerobic classes always use music. Music may facilitate our motivation to exercise, increase endurance, focus concentration, attend to chores,
and get in tune with our bodies. Some upbeat and fast-tempo music makes
us feel less tired. I always incorporate music in my hypnosis sessions and
on the self-hypnosis tapes and CDs I give my patients. Specifically designed hypnotic music is a component of the CD included with this book.

One way to select music that is best suited to you is to listen to a
variety of music styles. Record which types make you feel happy, sad,
energized, or relaxed. Then begin listening to these pieces when you feel
moody, and note your responses.

Healing with sound and chanting has been practiced since ancient
times. All forms of religion use music in their services. For thousands of
years, lullabies have assisted children in falling asleep.

Music that is used in combination with guided imagery facilitates psychological and spiritual growth. Psychosomatic disorders of all types, including headaches, digestive problems, pain, anxiety, and depression have
been successfully treated with music. Music enhances relaxation and learning, and aids the effectiveness of other consciousness-raising techniques.

Historical Applications of Hypnosis

Scholarly studies of various healing approaches from antiquity to the present reveal that the basis of hypnosis lies in what is called the alpha brain wave or "relaxation response."[1] Some degree of suggestion and/or hypnosis is used to bring about an altered state of consciousness (ASC), which provides the basis for healing.

Numerous references, dating back as far as 50,000 B.C., can be cited, from the exorcism of demons to the "ecstasy" states of the shamans. Chanting and breathing exercises were incorporated in early meditative rituals to achieve this alpha state. The Jewish Talmud relies on *Kavanah* to induce a state of focused concentration, relaxation, and correct intention.[2] In addition, these ASCs are found in the practices of Zen Buddhism, Sufism, Shintoism, Hinduism, Christian meditation, and yoga.

The ancient Chinese emphasized the importance of establishing balance and inner harmony between yin (darkness and death) and yang (light and life). Veith points out how the Chinese used visual imagery to heal the lower classes by confronting the "nether world of witches and wizardry, of animal disease and ancestral spirits, all of which can bring madness as well as cure."[3] By claiming to represent the positive yang energy, these priest-magicians were able to defeat the negative forces of yin.

Hypnosis, transcendental meditation, progressive relaxation, yoga, and autogenic training possess certain common characteristics that amount to a form of self-hypnosis, including:

- Eye fixation on a religious symbol or altar.
- A relaxing environment, often characterized by rhythmic music.
- A comfortable posture.
- Intonations of prayer.
- Rhythmic chanting.
- Self-contemplation.

A stone stele from the reign of the Egyptian pharaoh Ramses XII (approximately 3,000 years ago) makes reference to the demonic magical papyrus that contained detailed self-hypnotic techniques. MacHovec points out that the most thorough source of the ancient use of hypnosis is the Aesculapian priests, who first interpreted pilgrims' dreams and used a repetitive prayer to cast out these evil spirits. At other times, these priests used a brush to literally "brush away" the disease itself.[4]

Today, these sample principles are applied in psychotherapy in the form of guided affective imagery (GAI) and clinical hypnosis. Many New Age practitioners use soft music, the sound of wind chimes, or the chanting of mantras in darkened rooms surrounded by the scent of incense and other environmental settings to increase sensory awareness and establish a receptive condition that closely resembles the modern-day hypnotic state.

In applying visual imagery through hypnosis to resolve clinical and spiritual issues, we duplicate the various principles of suggestion and imagery originally practiced by saints, priests, and exorcists. This here-and-now approach is successful because it substitutes positive, constructive, healthy, and adaptive responses for negative, destructive, harmful, and maladaptive ones.

Suggestion

Suggestion can be divided into four distinct types. The first category, *verbal*, refers to communication produced by any type of sound. Second, *nonverbal* suggestion involves facial expressions and gestures. The third type is *intraverbal*, which refers to the vocal inflection and intonation of words. *Extraverbal* suggestion is the fourth and most powerful type and involves the implications of words and gestures; it uses appropriate gestures symbolic of the desired suggestion to influence the subject.

Suggestibility is a term applied to an act that is carried out uncritically, without the individual's logical processes participating in the response. Suggestibility is greatly enhanced whenever an individual repetitively hears any one of the four types of suggestions, either singularly or in combination. Rituals function to misdirect a subject's attention and facilitate his or her suggestibility. The degree of suggestibility depends not only on the techniques used to produce it, but also on expectations and other variables.

Another important variable is the quality of the relationship—that is, the rapport—established between therapist (or anyone giving suggestions) and subject.

The term *hypersuggestibility* is used to describe a state in which specific stimuli are responded to more readily as a result of the inhibition of competing ones. I must point out that increased suggestibility alone does not explain the complex processes associated with hypnotic behavior, even though increased suggestibility (hypersuggestibility) is a constant feature of hypnosis.

Principles of Hypnosis

Some general principles of hypnosis and its effect on behavior should be noted as you work with the exercises presented in this book.

1. Every Thought or Idea Produces a Physical Response.

Thoughts and ideas with strong emotional content produce physical responses in the body characteristic of the emotion. It has been clearly established that even the body's natural resistance to disease can be affected by a person's thoughts and emotions. To adapt successfully to the stresses of life and eliminate or change chronic negative physical reactions, we must first learn to change our thought patterns. We must learn to view situations positively. We must learn to change fixed, negative ideas into strong, positive attitudes. Such adaptation can be achieved through self-hypnosis and represents another example of our psychic empowerment.

2. What Is Imagined or Expected Tends to Be Realized.

When the subconscious mind perceives a goal, it automatically strives to achieve that goal. The individual who strongly believes in attaining a goal subconsciously strives to bring about favorable circumstances leading to this result. Expect good things, and good things will occur.

3. The Law of Reversed Effect.

The harder we try to accomplish something, the more difficult it is to obtain. Whenever a conflict exists between the will (conscious effort) and the imagination (mental imagery), not only do we not do that which we wish, but we do the exact opposite. When we think that we would like to do something but feel we cannot, the more we try, the more difficult it becomes. For example, the more we consciously try to remember a forgotten name, the more impossible it becomes. Later, when we have stopped trying and are thinking of something else, the name easily comes to mind.

4. New Habit Patterns Can Be Formed With Visualized Images.

The human nervous system cannot tell the difference between an actual experience and one that is vividly imagined. Habit patterns can be modified, and even reversed, simply by practicing or acting out the new response or behavior in the imagination.

5. Habit Patterns Can Be Performed With Autosuggestions.

Words are symbols that convey certain images and thoughts to the mind through previous associations. Once a word becomes associated with a specific image (object or action), the word alone then becomes a signal to the mind representative of that image and can act to elicit the same responses that the image itself would evoke. These words—in the form of suggestions—help the subconscious create the reality in which we live. Through the use of suggestions, we are able to create real situations corresponding to the goals we seek to achieve. Repetitious use of autosuggestions then act to form new patterns of behavior.

6. The Law of Dominant Effect.

When a suggestion is accompanied with a strong emotion, the strength of the suggestion is enhanced. Any previous suggestion will now be replaced by this suggestion-emotion combination.

A Self-Hypnosis Exercise

With this additional background, the following, more comprehensive progressive relaxation self-hypnosis exercise can be tried.

With your eyes closed, take a deep breath and hold it to the count of six. (Pause.) Let it out slowly and take a second deep breath, this time holding it to the count of eight. (Pause.) Let it out slowly once again.

Let all your muscles go loose and heavy. Just relax to the best of your ability. (Pause.) While the rest of your body continues to relax, I want you to create tension in your arms and fists by clenching them tighter and tighter. Breathing normally, just clench your fists and straighten your arms by stretching them in front of you, tighter and tighter. (Pause.) Feel the tension in your fists and arms while the rest of your body relaxes. Now let your hands and arms relax completely. Just let go and appreciate the relaxation.

Once again, clench your fists and straighten your arms. (Pause.) Now let go. Let your arms and hands relax, relaxing further and further on their own. Relax all over. (Pause.) Picture your hands and arms relaxing more and more. Your whole body is relaxing.

Now, while the rest of your body relaxes, I want you to point your toes away from your body, thereby tensing your feet and legs. Just point your toes away from your body, increasing the tension that way. Notice the tension in your leg muscles and feet; study the tension. (Pause.) Now, do the opposite. Relax. Let your feet and legs relax as completely as possible; appreciate the relaxation. Note the contrast between tension and relaxation in your legs and feet. (Pause.) Let the relaxation proceed on its own.

Now, point your feet in the other direction, creating tension that way. Once again notice the tension and study it. (Pause.) Relax your feet and legs now. Continue relaxing your legs further and further, the deeper relaxation spreading throughout your body.

Now concentrate your attention on the neck, head, and facial areas. While the rest of your body continues to relax on its own, press your head against the back of the chair. Notice the tension in your neck and the back of your head. (Pause.) Now, relax your head and neck. Let go of the tension. Note the relaxation in your neck and back of your head, your whole body relaxing more and more.

Now, once again, while the rest of your body relaxes, press your head against the back of the chair. Once again, feel the tension in your neck and head, notice the contrast between tension and relaxation. (Pause.) Now, stop the relaxation, let the relaxation continue on its own. Easing up, relaxing more and more all the time, deeper and deeper levels of relaxation all the time. Relaxing more and more automatically.

Now, let us remove any remaining tension in your facial area. Simply close your eyes tighter and tighter. As you do so, feel the tension created by stretching your forehead muscles. Notice this kind of tension; study it. Now, relax your eyes, ease up on the forehead. Just relax completely. Your eyes closed normally now. Let go, more and more, all over. (Pause.) Study the tension in your forehead, your eyes closed normally now. Feel the relaxation; you can just let the relaxation flow freely throughout your body. Relaxing now automatically as you gain the ability to just let your muscles switch off, switch off completely.

Now, to take you even deeper into relaxation, I want you simply to take in a really deep breath and hold it; concentrate any tiny bit of remaining tension in your chest area. (Pause.) Now, breathe out the tension; exhale completely. Relax and just breathe normally. Picture a relaxed feeling flowing throughout your entire body. Once again, take in a really deep breath and hold it while the rest of your body relaxes. Just notice the tension in your chest. (Pause.) Now, breathe out the tension. Just exhale automatically, and feel the ever-increasing waves of relaxation. Calm and serene and, more and more, totally at ease. Picture your whole body going deeper and deeper into relaxation. Stay in this relaxed state for five minutes.

All right now. You have done very well. Listen very carefully. I'm going to count forward now from one to five. When I reach the count of five you will be able to remember everything you experienced, and reexperienced. You'll feel very relaxed and refreshed; you'll be able to do whatever you have planned for the rest of the day or evening. You'll feel very positive about what you've just experienced and very motivated about your ability to achieve quicker and deeper relaxation with each exposure to self-hypnosis. All right now. One, very, very deep. Two, you're getting a little bit lighter. Three, you're getting much, much lighter. Four, very, very light. Five, awaken. Wide awake and refreshed.

To deepen this level of relaxation, try the following method.

With your eyes closed, I want you to let all of your muscles go loose and heavy. (Pause.) Loose and comfortably heavy. (Pause.) Simply let yourself relax to the very best of your ability, easing up all over now. (Pause.) Relaxing further and further all the time, I want you to take note of your breathing, listening only to the sound of my voice now, just notice that as you exhale, you become more comfortably relaxed. (Pause.) Each time you exhale, your whole body can become more and more deeply relaxed, calm, and serene. Easing up and relaxing, appreciating the deeper and deeper waves of relaxation. (Pause.) Relaxing more and more, comfortably heavy, comfortably warm and heavy. A pleasant, relaxed feeling as your whole body eases up all over. (Pause.)

Now, to help you go even deeper into relaxation, even further, I want you to picture yourself standing at the top of a long, long escalator, just watching the steps move down slowly in front of you. (Pause.) While you watch the steps move downward, notice that each time you breathe out, each time you exhale, you become automatically more relaxed. More and more deeply relaxed. Relaxing now as you watch the escalator stairs go down, down, down. (Pause.) As you watch the stairs go down, you go down deeper and deeper into relaxation, further and further.

Now, imagine yourself grasping the handrails of the escalator safely and securely. You step on the first stair. (Pause.) Now, you actually go down the escalator. As you go down the escalator, it becomes easier and easier to go more deeply into relaxation. Going deeper and deeper, all the time now, as you continue to ride the escalator down further and further. (Pause.) A pleasant, calm, serene feeling as you go still further. (Pause.) Deeper and deeper levels of relaxation automatically. Going with the relaxation freely and gently, just easing up all over more and more. (Pause.) Deeper and deeper levels of calm as you continue to ride the escalator down.

Now, while you continue to picture yourself riding down the escalator, safely and securely, I am going to help you achieve an even deeper calm, a deeper level of relaxation. (Pause.) Becoming more and more relaxed each time you breathe out, I am going to count from one to three, and on the count of three I want you to simply let your muscles switch off completely, thereby doubling your present state of relaxation. (Pause.) One, (pause) two, (pause) and three. Doubly down now, doubly relaxed down even further now and further. (Pause.) It's easier and easier to become more and more fully relaxed, calm, and serene, more and more totally at ease. A pleasant, comfortable, heavy feeling as you go all the way down now, all the way, a pleasant, comfortably warm, relaxed feeling.

All right now. You have done very well. Listen very carefully. I'm going to count forward now from one to five. When I reach the count of five, you will be able to remember everything you experienced, and reexperienced, you'll feel very relaxed and refreshed; you'll be able to do whatever you have planned for the rest of the day or evening. You'll feel very positive about what you've just experienced and very motivated about your confidence and ability to get quicker and deeper with each exposure to self-hypnosis. All right now. One, very, very deep. Two, you're getting a little bit lighter. Three, you're getting much, much lighter. Four, very, very light. Five, awaken. Wide awake and refreshed.

Subconscious Resistance to Suggestions

Fear is the largest obstacle to entering into hypnosis and accepting suggestions. Learning as much as possible about just what this natural alpha state is all about both adds to our desire to enter hypnosis and facilitates our success in using it to increase our ability to attain any goal humanly possible.

It is through suggestions that you specify your goals and direct the subconscious to the achievement of those goals. The subconscious mind does not know the difference between reality and imagination. This is because the subconscious mind is limited to deductive logic—the process of reasoning from the general to the specific. A useful suggestion repeated often enough and long enough will be accepted by the subconscious mind as true. If the suggestion is formulated correctly, and if it is not of a nature to trigger much resistance, it will work.

You cannot simply induce hypnosis on yourself quickly, state a couple of suggestions, and expect major changes to take place. Emile Coué stated it best during the early 1900s: "Every day, in every way, I am getting better and better." The subconscious does have a natural tendency to resist change because of its programming from the conscious mind. There is an attitude of acceptance for change at the subconscious level. This is the window of possibility, the amount of change that the subconscious will find acceptable at any given time. If you confine your change efforts to these windows, you will note they trigger subconscious resistance. Once the change you want is in place, the subconscious now accepts more changes and you can start working on the next level within your range of goals. In this manner, you work your way up to the next level of your goal mountain one plateau at a time rather than try to soar to the top all at once. Think of it in terms of degrees of change. Your suggestions should be directed toward raising the limits that your subconscious mind finds acceptable and the behaviors that lead to your goals.

Is Hypnosis Dangerous?

Our consumer culture bombards us with various forms of advertising that can have a hypnotic effect. Advertisers may even pay a premium for broadcasting late at night or early in the morning, when people are more likely to be highly suggestible. Learning about hypnosis and suggestibility helps us recognize times when we may be more open or vulnerable so that we can retain awareness and have more control.

Fear is by far the greatest obstacle to experiencing hypnosis. The late Milton Erickson demonstrated that no scientific evidence exists that hypnosis weakens a person's will or renders it any more dependent than any other therapeutic technique.[5] There is absolutely no danger in a hypnotized individual acting out fantasies that conflict with his or her moral or ethnical code. During the past 175 years of scientific research involving hypnosis, not one case has demonstrated any harm resulting from the hypnotic trance. Based on past history and on my own clinical experience with more than 14,000 individual patients since 1974, I can state with absolute certainly that *hypnosis is not dangerous*.

CHAPTER 2

ELIMINATE
UNWANTED HABITS

Before presenting detailed scripts for using self-hypnosis to remove unwanted habits, let's discuss how to prepare hypnotic suggestions and visual imagery techniques.

Rules for Formulating Suggestions

1. Always word your instructions positively. Positive suggestions are more likely to be accepted by the subconscious compared with negative ones. For example, saying, "I am steadily losing weight every week," is far better than saying, "I am not fat."

2. Repeat suggestions frequently to maximize effect; however, avoid using clichés.

3. Personalize suggestions to deal specifically with current goals. For example, you might say, "I am steadily losing my desire for doughnuts and candy, and will substitute fruits for them by Friday." Use the term *I*, not *you*. For example, don't say "you are," say "I am."

4. Use a detailed and logical approach in formatting suggestions. If your goal can be quantified, suggest a precise improvement. It is far more effective to say, "I am steadily losing weight every day to reach my ideal weight of 115 pounds," than, "I will lose weight."

35

5. Ensure that all suggestions are clear, simple, and, whenever possible, in the present tense. Never refer to past conditions, and use the progressive form of the present tense to bypass the critical conscious mind. For example, it is more effective to state, "Every day my mind and body are working together to eliminate my desire for processed sugar," than, "I will get thinner."

6. Use visualizations, and attach words that depict emotions, such as *vibrant, sparkling, thrilling, wonderful, powerful, radiant, loving, generous, exciting, delightful,* and *beautiful.* The more vivid and dramatic the image, the more effective it will be because visualizations are suggestions.

Rules for Administering Hypnotic Suggestion

1. Use the previous section as a guide and write out your suggestions.
2. Edit these thoughts to apply to current goals.
3. Read these suggestions aloud and complete your revisions.
4. Make a tape of these suggestions using the scripts presented later in this chapter and in subsequent chapters. Using self-hypnosis tapes is by far the easiest and most efficient way to practice self-hypnosis. If you are making your own tapes from these models, substitute the term *I* for *you* in these scripts. To construct your own tapes inexpensively and quickly, please refer to my book *New Age Hypnosis* for further details.

The Hypnotic Environment

The room in which you practice self-hypnosis should be subdued in lighting and a few degrees warmer than room temperature, with no drafts. The walls, floors, drapes, and rugs should not be distracting. Make sure the room is quiet and free from offending odors. If you are sitting, make sure that your back is supported against the back of the chair. Your feet should be flat on the floor or on a footrest. Knees and ankles should not be crossed. Hands should rest on the arms of the chair, on your thighs, or loosely in your lap. Your head should be in a comfortable position.

To practice self-hypnosis, it is preferable to use a recliner rather than a bed or couch, which are associated with sleep. If you are reclining, your arms should be alongside your body and your head should be slightly elevated. Feet should be separated with toes turned outward. Use headphones to listen to your tapes, and keep a blanket by your side. A tape of metronome beats is ideal for pacing your voice and inducing hypnosis. Loosen clothing and remove shoes.

Allow 20 minutes to 30 minutes for each practice session. It is beneficial to add brief, hypnotic experiences spaced throughout the day. This is called *fractionation*, and it is a powerful relaxation technique. The deeper your level of relaxation, the deeper the trance.

Any self-improvement requires disciplined practice. The more you practice, the easier self-hypnosis becomes. The more practiced and highly skilled you become, the greater the benefits. By using self-hypnosis regularly, you can bring forward inner resources with greater ease. When the mind and body work together, both consciously and unconsciously, you are on the road to health, success, and personal empowerment.

The following are some additional recommendations for making and using self-hypnosis tapes:

- Set a regular time each day to play your tapes.
- If you want to take a more active part in your tape session, sit up in bed or in a chair, and lie down only after the session is finished.
- In making a bedtime tape, do not include a wake-up section. Simply make the suggestion to go right into your natural sleep cycle from the hypnotic state.
- It is quite natural for the conscious mind to wander during self-hypnosis. Do not be concerned that you may be wasting your time when this happens. In addition, you may experience hypnoamnesia (lack of memory), and this signifies a fairly deep level of hypnosis. Your conscious mind's activities and/or state of boredom are irrelevant to your use of self-hypnosis. The only concern is the subconscious.
- I highly recommend adding music at open spaces throughout the tape. This deepens the trance level and blocks out distracting environmental noises. The total time, including

the music, should not exceed 30 minutes, though 20 minutes is preferred.

+ Responses to identical words presented by the same person in an identical manner vary widely from one person to another.

+ Anyone who can speak and read with reasonable freedom can induce hypnosis. Absolutely everyone can be hypnotized to a greater extent.

+ Words have power in that they produce ideas in the minds of the listeners. The acceptance of certain ideas constitutes hypnosis. Hypnotic programming works by repeated exposure.

+ The power of hypnosis resides with the person being hypnotized, not the hypnotist.

+ Do not try too hard to enter into self-hypnosis. A vigorous effort to be hypnotized prevents a successful response as much as strong resistance.

+ A permissive suggestion is more likely to be carried out than a dominating command.

+ You cannot be forced to do anything as a result of hypnosis that you would not usually do.

+ You must be motivated to overcome the difficulty of which you complain. It is possible to increase motivation by suggestion.

+ Work on one issue at a time.

+ If a posthypnotic suggestion is used (most therapeutic suggestions are posthypnotic), always incorporate a cue for terminating the suggestion if it should be ended. For example, when I say "sleep now and rest," you will automatically detach yourself from any visualization and await further instructions.

+ If the posthypnotic suggestion should not be terminated, be careful not to inadvertently give a cue for termination. If I wanted a patient to elaborate on a visualization, I would say "sleep now and rest" to deepen the trance.

+ You will remember everything that you experience during a trance, unless you are a very deep-level subject.

+ The more determined you are to attain a goal, the greater your chances of success.

Muscle Relaxation

The principle behind muscle relaxation in mind-body approaches is that whatever relaxes your muscles will also relax your mind. Tensing and relaxing each muscle group one at a time will result in a progressive relaxation of your entire body, while at the same time calming the mind.

For this exercise you are going to tense each muscle group for five seconds and focus on this sensation. This is followed by breathing deeply and immediately releasing this tension so the muscle goes completely limp. At this time, observe the difference between the tense sensation and the relaxed state for 20 seconds. Each muscle group is to be tensed and relaxed twice.

1. Lie on your back on a soft surface. Now clench your left fist and keep it tense for five seconds. Notice the feeling in all the muscles of your fingers, hand, and forearm.

2. Breath deeply and immediately relax your hand and arm. Notice the looseness in your right hand, and compare this sensation to the previous tensed one for 20 seconds.

3. Repeat these steps once again and do this same exercise with the right hand.

4. Now repeat steps 1 through 3 with your arms and upper arms.

5. Straighten your thigh muscles and press your heels against the surface beneath them. Repeat steps 1 to 3.

6. Tense your calf muscles by pointing your toes down and curling them. Repeat steps 1 to 3.

7. Now bend your toes up toward your head and produce tension in your shin region. Repeat steps 1 to 3.

8. Pull your stomach in and hold it for five seconds. Repeat steps 1 to 3.

9. Squeeze your buttocks together for five seconds. Repeat steps 1 to 3.

10. Now repeat these procedures with your shoulders by shrugging them, pressing your shoulder blades together and arching your back.

11. Press your head back as far as you comfortably can, hold, then relax.

12. Now pull your chin down as if attempting to touch your chest, hold, then relax.

13. Use movements such as wrinkling your forehead, frowning, closing your eyes tightly, wrinkling your nose, clenching your jaws, pressing your tongue against the roof of your mouth and pursing your lips. Always repeat steps 1 to 3.

When you complete this exercise with two repetitions, feel the complete sensation of relaxation permeating your entire body. Savor this feeling and take several long, deep breaths just before getting up. This procedure allows you to quickly scan the body, locate tense areas, and relax them.

Overcoming Procrastination

To eliminate any unwanted habit, procrastination must first be removed from behavior. If you have the time to do something but simply put it off, you are exhibiting procrastination. Feelings of guilt and being overwhelmed with responsibilities often accompany procrastination. Procrastination is far more than mere inefficient time management. It also involves the self-image.

Although procrastinators are well known for being indecisive, the dynamics of the merely indecisive differ from those of procrastinators. Two main types of procrastination can be identified. Trait procrastination is characterized by a deep personality disorder that is commonly exhibited, whereas in state procrastination, the individual only occasionally puts off responsibilities. A continuum exists between state and trait procrastination, with most people falling somewhere in the middle.

A Self-Hypnosis Exercise

The following self-hypnosis script may be helpful in overcoming any form of procrastination you may be exhibiting.

You are persistent, determined, and ambitious. You complete each task because you are a success-oriented winner. You fulfill each personal and professional desire in a relentless, yet efficient and empowering way. You have the self-discipline to accomplish all of your personal and professional goals. Each day that passes will result in an increase in your self-discipline. You can now complete large and complicated tasks by breaking them down into smaller components and doing each job one step at a time.

You are clear and focused on your values and have no reservations about committing to your goals. You remain alert and focused on what you are doing. You can routinely block out all thoughts except those related to what you are doing. You are a winner and will now always exhibit a success-type personality. You are self-reliant and self-confident.

You are filled with independence and determination. You project a highly positive self-image and can do whatever you set your mind to. You evaluate the various factors of a goal objective and decide what you want. You have the courage and inner strength to make and carry out life-changing decisions. You do what you say you will do. You finish what you start. You fulfill your commitments. You do it today, not tomorrow. You have the power and ability to do more in less time. You use a schedule and make it work for you. You increase your speed and productivity. You finish your projects. You now speak up and say what you want to say. It is easy to say what needs to be said. You stand up for yourself and increase your self-esteem. You will not tolerate manipulation.

You have the power and ability to create any reality you desire, especially one free from procrastination.

Visual Imagery

Throughout this chapter, the focus is on using simple self-hypnosis exercises to permanently remove undesirable habits. Visual imagery is an important component to these techniques. To fully appreciate this approach, a discussion of visual imagery is necessary.

The mind can literally create reality through the effective use of visual imagery; however, it must be consistent. Visualizing yourself as a nonsmoker but complaining about nicotine stains on your fingers or the odor of smoke in your clothes nullifies any progress toward your goal to give up smoking.

Research has frequently demonstrated the positive effects of visual imagery in stimulating sexual arousal, lowering blood pressure, slowing down heart rates, stimulating the immune system, and so on. In addition, imagery can assist in uncovering the etiology of unwanted habits and bringing to light solutions to these dysfunctional behaviors.

A little background concerning the way the brain works will help illustrate this concept. For right-handed individuals, the left brain controls understanding and language, as well as writing and speaking. It is the analytical and logical component of the brain.

The right brain concerns itself with spatial relationships, feelings, creativity, pictures, and sounds. The right brain pieces together the data collected by the left brain. Thus, the left brain processes information sequentially, whereas the right brain processes it simultaneously. The opposite is true for left-handed people.

Right-handed people use this big-picture function of the right brain to apply visual-imagery techniques. I describe this innate ability as *global assessment*. By assembling the data gathered by the analytical and logical left brain, the right brain globally assesses new solutions to old problems (and may uncover opportunities previously ignored).

Through imagery, you can learn to relax and be more comfortable in any situation. Imagery can be used to help you tap inner strengths, and to find hope, courage, patience, perseverance, love, and other qualities that can help you eliminate the cause of unwanted habits.

Conditions that are caused or aggravated by stress, such as anxiety, often respond successfully to imagery techniques. The emotional aspects of any habit can often be controlled through imagery, and relieving the emotional distress may, in turn, encourage you to become more empowered and permanently resolve the issue.

Relaxation techniques are the first step in learning to use your images, thoughts, and feelings skillfully. The ability to quiet the mind and concentrate attention enables you to make the most effective use of any technique. Self-hypnosis is by far the most efficient method in attaining a relaxed state.

Learning to relax is fundamental to self-healing and a prerequisite for using imagery effectively. Relaxation is a first exercise in focusing and concentrating your mind on the process of healing. In addition, deep physiologic relaxation has health benefits of its own. It allows your body to channel its energy into repair and restoration, and provides respite from habitual patterns of tension.

Active imagery communicates conscious intentions (or requests) to the subconscious mind. It is a simple process that consists of imagining a desired goal as if it is already achieved, while maintaining a passive, relaxed state of mind.

Frequency of practice seems to be a particularly important factor in effectiveness. People who practice using visualization techniques most frequently and enthusiastically receive the greatest benefit. So when you begin to use imagery, do so often and wholeheartedly. You may think of imagery as an affirmation, a suggestion that begins to lead you in the desired direction. Even if you don't experience relief right away, be patient and consistent as you imagine the process as vividly as you can.

A Self-Hypnosis Exercise

Make use of the following visual imagery exercise to increase your self-confidence.

> *Sit comfortably, relax, and breathe deeply. Visualize yourself in your favorite serene environment—it may be the beach, a park, or a cabin in the woods. Add to this the sounds of nature and the time of year you enjoy most.*

> *Imagine walking along in your favorite surroundings while looking up at the sky. Notice that a rainbow has appeared and focus your attention on the colors. You see red, yellow, blue, green, orange, purple, and violet.*

As you stare at this rainbow, realize that you can accomplish anything you want to as long as you can see the rainbow. The rainbow doesn't need to be present for you to accomplish your goal; however, if it is there, it ensures a successful outcome to any quest.

Sit down now and think of the kind of person you would like to become. Review personality traits, health issues, finances, and relationships. Focus on specific goals and aspects of your personality. Look up again and see the rainbow. You are now able to accomplish the goal of becoming who you want to be.

Imagine a large television screen in front of you. Project the ideal you on the right side of this large TV. Then, project an image of how you are on the left side. This is called a split-screen effect. Imagine yourself adjusting the fine-tuning knobs. As you adjust the TV, the ideal image of you becomes crystal clear, while the current image of you goes out of focus and then disappears completely. Look up one more time and note the presence of the rainbow. The ideal image of you is now your new reality. Meditate on this image for at least five minutes with soothing New Age music playing in the background.

Finally, breathe deeply, open your eyes, and say, "I am confident. I am in charge of my life, and I now claim my power to improve my confidence level every day."

End your trance as usual.

Use this model for all exercises. Another popular and successful approach is what I refer to as the *sanctuary method*. Most people can relate to a pleasant or favorite place. This can be some place you have been, or somewhere you might like to go. Let yourself enjoy this place as much as you would like. (For example, some people think of a time when they went to the beach or ocean. They can almost hear the waves hitting the shore, feel the warmth of the sun and the gentle breezes, smell the salty air, and so forth.) As you enjoy the image, let yourself relax deeper and deeper. Therapeutic suggestions can be made as you continue to enjoy this favorite place.

A Visual-Imagery Exercise

The following is a script that uses visual imagery of the sanctuary method to assist in reducing anxiety.

You now have the ability to learn to remain calm, peaceful, tranquil, and relaxed through the power of your mind, and it is ultimately your mind that will enable you to attain any goal by eliminating your previous anxiety responses to the world around you. You will find that the words CALM, PEACEFUL, TRANQUIL, and RELAXED will help your mind and body to unwind and become calm; you will develop a feeling of being tension free whenever you say these four words, CALM, PEACEFUL, TRANQUIL, and RELAXED.

Now, I want you to think of a place where you find mental peace and quiet; it may be a place with trees, mountains, water; it may be a meadow, a lake, a stream, the ocean; and it may be the summer, spring, winter, or fall. Notice the smallest details of this sanctuary—the colors and textures; or perhaps you can hear the sound and smell the scents that you associate with this place; or perhaps you can feel the calm, peace, tranquility, and relaxation that you associate with it. Now, as your conscious mind becomes more and more involved with your quiet place, allow your subconscious mind to help you to maximize this feeling of complete relaxation. Do this now.

PLAY NEW AGE MUSIC FOR THREE MINUTES.

Anytime you have feelings of apprehension, all you need to do is take a deep breath, and when you exhale say to yourself, "calm, peaceful, tranquil, relaxed." You will feel your mood change as a feeling of inner calm comes over your body.

If you experience any apprehension or anxiety whatsoever, take a deep breath, and when you exhale say the words, "calm, peaceful, tranquil, relaxed." Allow yourself to float, to enter a state of mind in which nothing disturbs you.

End your trance as usual.

Insomnia Exercise—A Self-Hypnosis Exercise

For those suffering from insomnia, the following is a simple self-hypnosis exercise that can be practiced to both relax you and promote a good night's rest.

Resting in your bed with your eyes closed, take a deep breath and hold it to the count of six. (Pause.) Let it out slowly and take a second deep breath, this time holding it to the count of eight. (Pause.) Let it out slowly once again.

Let all your muscles go loose and heavy. Just relax to the best of your ability. (Pause.) Now, while the rest of your body continues to relax, I want you to create tension in your arms and fists by clenching your fists tighter and tighter. Breathing normally, clench your fists tighter and tighter, and straighten your arms by stretching them in front of you. (Pause.) Feel the tension in your fists and arms, while the rest of your body relaxes. Now, let your hands and arms relax completely. Just let go and appreciate the relaxation.

Once again, clench your fists and straighten your arms. Notice the tension, while the rest of your body relaxes. (Pause.) Now let go, let your arms and hands relax, relaxing further and further on their own. Relaxing all over. (Pause.) Picture your hands and arms relaxing more and more; your whole body relaxing.

Now, while the rest of your body relaxes, I want you to point your toes away from your body, thereby tensing your feet and legs. Point your toes away from your body, increasing the tension that way. Notice the tension in your leg muscles and feet; study the tension. (Pause.) And now do the opposite. Relax. Let your feet and legs relax as completely as possible; appreciate the relaxation. Note the contrast between tension and relaxation in your legs and feet. (Pause.) Let the relaxation proceed on its own.

Now, pull your toes upward, creating tension that way. Once again, notice the tension and study it. (Pause.) Relax your feet and legs now. Just continue relaxing your legs further and further, allowing the deeper relaxation to spread throughout your body.

Now, concentrate attention on the neck, head, and facial areas. While the rest of your body continues to relax on its own, press your head against the back of the bed. Notice the tension in your neck and the back of your head. (Pause.) And now relax your head and neck. Let go of the tension and relax.

As you count backward now from seven to one, each muscle in your body will become completely relaxed. Seven; deeper, deeper, six; deeper, deeper, five; deeply relaxed; four; three; two; so deeply relaxed, one. Now, you are in a deep level of hypnosis and are going deeper into this naturally relaxed state with each breath you exhale.

As you exhale each breath, you are going to program your subconscious mind to have the most comfortable and restful night's sleep you have ever experienced. Your sleep will be undisturbed throughout the night unless a true emergency arises, in which case you will awaken immediately. In the absence of an emergency, you will awaken at the appropriate time you desire the following morning and this new sleep routine will be a part of your new reality. Now sleep, sleep, sleep.

Weight Reduction

Americans—about 60 percent of whom are overweight, and approximately 35 percent who qualify as obese—turn to diets to lose weight. More than half of the nation is dieting or has dieted. But has this system of dieting worked?

During the past 40 years, Americans have been on thousands of diets. These diets obviously don't work permanently; they are only temporary measures that produce temporary results. Permanent measures result in permanent changes.

Diets fail for many reasons. For example, most dieters focus on what they are going to eat when their ordeal is finally over. How can you possibly succeed on a diet when all you are thinking about is food? Depriving yourself is not the answer to healthy, permanent weight loss. It usually causes you to binge later on, which complicates this problem. Deprivation and bingeing become a vicious cycle, and that's just one of the many problems with dieting.

Through the proper use of self-hypnosis, old patterns can be unlearned, and new and healthier ways of eating can be learned. This approach also trains you to handle all the tensions and frustrations of daily life, without resorting to fattening foods. All you need is the proper motivation to accomplish this goal.

A Self-Hypnosis Exercise

Now, you are ready for self-image building suggestions. Try using the following script.

An average body weight is very desirable to you. You will now eat a healthy diet in amounts required to maintain an average body weight for your height and frame. You now resolve conflicts directly, not through the way your body looks.

You have the inner strength and determination to overcome any past tendencies to manifest any type of eating disorder. You will now project a positive self-image, feel balanced and fulfilled, and view life as a tranquil oneness. This will include your own body image.

You love yourself and believe in yourself. Every day, in every way, you are becoming empowered and permanently removing all causes and factors that led to the previous negative eating habits. You absolutely desire this new state of mind, free of all eating problems and reaching and maintaining your ideal weight and body image. You can create your own positive new reality.

Trigger Zones

Before presenting a detailed script for weight reduction, I will first discuss situations to which most people react by overeating. I refer to these as *trigger zones*. The best way to understand these trigger zones is to write down and enumerate every situation that you associate with habitual, compulsive, or emotional eating. I am not referring to physiological hunger, just psychological stimuli to eat.

Common examples of trigger zones include:

+ Being very busy (grabbing a quick snack on the run).
+ Confronting food situations (preparing foods, supermarket shopping, seeing and smelling tasty, fattening foods).
+ Relaxing (watching television, entertaining company at home, coming home from work or school).
+ During routine activities (reading the paper, housework, driving, bookkeeping).
+ Staying away from home (eating in restaurants, cocktail parties, visiting friends or relatives).
+ Coping with mood swings (boredom, worrying, during or following a crisis, as a tranquilizer, at the end of a trying day, being frustrated by discovering you haven't lost weight).

The next step is to design a healthy resolution to each trigger zone and prepare specific suggestions to resolve that issue. Finding something more constructive that you can do instead of eating improper foods is your goal with this exercise.

Bear in mind that you will not be able to resolve all issues at once; however, constant repetition of these suggestions will eventually result in a conditioned response that will obviate your need to recall them to mind daily.

A Self-Hypnosis Exercise

Now, try this rather comprehensive script before moving on to the visualization exercises.

Being overweight is unhealthy.

You need your body to live.

You owe your body this respect and protection.

You have the power to reprogram your subconscious mind to reverse previous thoughts of overeating and thinking of yourself as being overweight. You will, starting today, reprogram your subconscious to think of yourself as being thin, and eat only the foods that are healthy and necessary for your body.

You are going to lose all the weight that you desire to lose, and you are going to do this starting today. I want you to associate this relaxed state that you are now in with a relaxed attitude about losing weight. Don't count calories. As you lose weight, you will gain more confidence and find further weight reduction easier. When you eat, you will cut your food into small pieces and chew them slowly and completely before swallowing. Eat only one mouthful of food at a time. You will find that by eating slowly, and in smaller portions, you will enjoy your meals more and eat less food. You will find that halfway through a meal you will feel full. When this happens you will stop eating. You will never, ever eat when you are not hungry.

Repeat these statements to yourself:

- *I will get more filling satisfaction from less food every day.*
- *I will eat slowly and only at mealtimes, sparingly and properly.*
- *I am losing weight steadily every week.*
- *I am becoming slim and shapely.*
- *I have a stronger feeling every day that I am in complete control of my eating habits.*
- *I am developing a greater liking every day for the foods that make me slim and shapely.*

Remember, if you repeatedly deny satisfaction to a hunger pang, the desire eventually goes away.

From this moment on, you will not think of yourself as being overweight. Every time such a thought comes into your mind, it programs your subconscious negatively. So you will now monitor your thoughts. Any thoughts or actions that come to mind about being overweight will be canceled out by saying to yourself, "I am thin, I am thin." From this moment on, you are going to eat only those foods that are necessary to keep you healthy and mentally alert. You are going to eat smaller portions of the foods necessary to keep you mentally alert and healthy. You will desire no more.

You will be totally aware of eating; you will no longer eat by habit. From this moment on, you will no longer eat between meals or while watching TV, and you will have absolutely no desire to eat between meals or while watching TV.

You are going to set a realistic goal for your excess weight loss, and you will carry it out successfully. Decide how many pounds you can realistically lose every week, and you will lose this exact amount. Now, repeat to yourself the realistic amount of weight that you can lose each week until you reach your ideal weight of _____ pounds.

You will find it easier and easier every day to stick to a reducing diet. You will enjoy smaller meals. The irritation and annoyances of everyday life are rolling off you like water off a duck's back. You will thoroughly enjoy the foods that are healthy.

Some people fear being thin. But you don't have to fear losing weight. No matter why you gained weight, for whatever reasons you became a compulsive eater, it is no longer important. What is important is that you have decided to change your eating habits so that you can reach your desired goal—the image, shape, weight, and size that you desire. It doesn't really come into account whether you are fat or become thin. You are still the same person. You still have the same power, the same personality, the same inner reality—no matter what your body shape, weight, or size is. You need not fear losing any of yourself when you lose weight. As the weight and inches roll off, as you control your eating habits, you remain the same you, only more trim. You do not need to fear that you are losing any of your protection. You are the same person.

If you want to be someone different, don't wait until you lose all the weight to be become the person you want to be. Wear the clothes now that project your image. Sit, walk, and act with your thin personality. Don't worry about hiding the fat. Wearing fat clothes doesn't hide the fat. They only make you feel worse. So wear the clothes that you want to wear, that project the real you, now, as you are losing weight. This will reinforce your desire to reach your goal.

As the extra weight begins to roll off, to melt away, to disappear, you are totally comfortable with your emerging slender and shapely body. You are perfectly content and at ease with the emerging slim, trim, and slender you. You are in control of your eating habits. You are in control of your life. You are in control of losing weight, and you are in control of your personality and your body. And you are perfectly happy with the inner you that remains as you lose weight and inches.

You truly believe that you are capable of dieting successfully and effortlessly to achieve and maintain your ideal weight of _____pounds. You will be guided by the natural powers within you to achieve and maintain this healthy and attractive body.

Whenever you are tempted to eat fattening food or to violate any of these suggestions, you will automatically ask yourself if you really want to indulge. If you do want to indulge, you will; however, you will find that you prefer to exercise the hypnotic techniques and suggestions to reach and maintain your ideal weight.

A Visual-Imagery Exercise

This next exercise uses visual imagery to assist you in perceiving your ideal body image, free of weight problems.

Mentally see an image of yourself standing before you. This is your body exactly as you would like it to appear, free of any and all negative eating behavior. Examine it more and more closely now, and it will be a realistic (but ideal) body image, one that you really can achieve, and one that you will achieve. And when you have a clear image of your body as you would like it, keep observing that image, and make it a part of your own reality.

PLAY NEW AGE MUSIC FOR TWO MINUTES.

That ideal body image is becoming more and more real. You are seeing it clearly, and in its full size and dimensions. And now you are going to step forward and into that body. You will find yourself in that body, so that you can try it out and make certain that it is just the body you do want to have. And if you would like to change something, make those changes now. Visualize yourself free of all desires to overeat. Picture yourself at your ideal weight.

Move around in that body, feel its strength and agility, its dynamic aliveness, its surging vitality, and make really certain that its appearance and all its attributes are what you realistically desire. And as you occupy that body, and come to know that body very well, your present physical body is going to be drawn in that new mold. You are moving already toward the realization of that ideal body image, and you will be doing whatever is needed to achieve that body you want to have. You are completely free of all negative eating tendencies.

PLAY NEW AGE MUSIC FOR FOUR MINUTES.

All right. Sleep now and rest. You did very, very well. Listen very carefully. I'm going to count forward now from one to five. When I reach the count of five, you will be able to remember everything you experienced and reexperienced. You'll feel very relaxed and refreshed, and you'll be able to do whatever you have planned for the rest of the day or evening. You'll feel very positive about what you've just experienced and very motivated about your confidence and ability to play this tape again to experience self-hypnosis. All right now. One, very, very deep. Two, you're getting a little bit lighter. Three, you're getting much, much lighter. Four, very, very light. Five, awaken. Wide awake and refreshed.

A Visual-Imagery Exercise

The following visual-imagery script will further enhance your subconscious programming to attain your ideal weight.

Imagine yourself at your ideal weight. See a friend or mate shopping with you. Your friend is amazed at your thin appearance. Now, visualize two tables in front of you. The table on the right has all the foods you like that add unwanted weight. List examples of these foods. Now draw a large red X through the table and imagine looking at yourself in a sideshow mirror (one that makes you look very wide and short).

The table on the left contains food that is healthy and will not add unwanted weight—for example, fish, eggs, and lean meats, and fruits and vegetables. Now, draw a large yellow check mark through the table and imagine looking at yourself in a mirror that makes you appear tall and thin. Mentally tell yourself that you desire only foods on the check-marked table. Imagine your friends, family, and parents telling you how great you look by (specify a date), weighing only (specify an amount). Visualize a photograph of yourself at your ideal weight.

Visualize a photograph of yourself at your present weight. Now, focus on the photograph of yourself at your ideal weight. The other photograph disappears. Imagine how it will feel at your ideal weight to bend over to tie your shoelace, walk, jog, or wear a bathing suit on the beach.

Now, mentally select an ideal diet that will help you reach your ideal weight. Tell yourself that this is all the food your body will need or desire, and it will not send hunger pangs for more.

PLAY NEW AGE MUSIC FOR FOUR MINUTES.

End your trance as usual.

When you regularly incorporate mental pictures into your self-hypnosis regimen, you will begin to notice success in your behavioral changes and positive attitude. In my Los Angeles office, I work with many celebrities and highly successful corporate executives. One common trait I find among these patients is that they have all imagined themselves attaining success before realizing their goals.

The proper and repeated use of mental movies will eventually eliminate your old, negative self-image, and replace it with one that embraces everything you desire. You must reinforce these images by actual practice in your daily life, but visualization is the first step to reaching and maintaining your ideal weight permanently and naturally.

It is essential that you have proper eating patterns and a clear mental picture of how you wish to look. Keep this image uppermost in your mind from the beginning of your use of self-hypnosis, until your subconscious is reprogrammed.

Smoking

When dealing with such habits as smoking, nail biting, alcoholism, and grinding one's teeth (bruxism), it is best to become aware of engaging in this unwanted habit the moment it is about to manifest. Gradual reduction of these habits is easier and psychologically less threatening than immediate cessation.

A Self-Hypnosis Exercise

Try the following script to eliminate smoking.

> *You will have more self-control in the future. You will be able to smoke, if you wish to smoke, and you will be able to not smoke, if you wish not to smoke. You will realize that smoking is a form of irritation and that the longer you go without a cigarette the less need you will have to smoke. One hour from now you will have less interest in smoking than you feel at this time. Two hours from now you will have less interest in smoking than you will have one hour from now. Thus, as each hour goes by, you will have less interest, less desire, and less need to smoke.*

You have the utmost respect for your body. Smoking is a poison. You need your body to live. You owe your body this respect and protection.

You will be aware of smoking each time you light up a cigarette. You will no longer smoke by habit. You will weigh the advantages and disadvantages of smoking each time you are thinking about a cigarette.

You will ignore the desire to smoke. Do not think about not smoking or smoking at all. If you repeatedly deny dissatisfaction to any urge by ignoring it, the urge eventually goes away.

From now on, you will not smoke one-half hour after awakening in the morning, before breakfast, and within one-half hour after meals, and one-half hour before bed (lengthen this time as progress is made). You will brush your teeth and use mouthwash at these times. The clean, fresh taste in your mouth is desirable, and you will want to do everything possible to maintain this state.

Each cigarette that you smoke will give you less and less pleasure. Associate this relaxation that you have now with a control over your own body through the use of your subconscious mind. You are steadily losing your desire for cigarettes.

By giving up smoking, you will improve your health. You will be less likely to suffer from heart disease, emphysema, bronchitis, and lung cancer. Your digestion will improve, and your food will taste better; however, you will not overeat because your self-confidence will improve as well.

Hold your breath for a slow count of 10. Let your breath out slowly and note how relaxed you are inhaling this fresh, smokeless air. You will continue to be more relaxed as you breathe out fresh, smokeless air. You are in complete control of all your habits. If the desire to smoke should arise, say to yourself, "I no longer smoke, and I don't need to smoke." The annoyances and irritation of everyday life are rolling off you like water off a duck's back.

Nicotine is a poison. Smoking is harmful to everyone's health; this is an established fact. Excessive smoking increases nervous tension...it doesn't decrease it.

Anyone can stop smoking...you have the power to stop smoking permanently. Whenever you are tempted to smoke, you will automatically ask yourself if you really want to indulge yourself. If you do want to indulge, you will; however, you will find that you prefer to exercise the hypnotic techniques and suggestions that I have given you to eliminate the cause, desire, and need for smoking cigarettes.

A Visual-Imagery Exercise

Now, try this visual-imagery exercise to visualize yourself as a nonsmoker.

You are a free and powerful being who, beginning today, will eliminate once and for all any desire to smoke. Your body and mind will heal and balance itself. You have all of the inner strength necessary to create your new reality free of smoking.

You are in control of your life and are confident about your ability to permanently eliminate smoking from your reality. Every day, you are programming your subconscious to accomplish this goal.

You unconditionally love and accept yourself and deserve to free yourself of smoking. You have the self-discipline to accomplish your personal and professional goals. Every day, in every way, you increase your self-discipline. You do what you need to do, and stop doing what doesn't work. You now adapt and keep pace with movements of change. You always consider your options, and you always act in your own best interests. You are self-reliant and self-confident. You are filled with independence and determination. You project a positive self-image. You can do whatever you set your mind to.

Mentally see an image of yourself standing before you. This is your body exactly as you would like it to appear, free of any and all desire to smoke. Examine it more and more closely now, and it will be a realistic but ideal body image, one that you really can achieve, and one that you will achieve. And when you have a very clear image of your body as you would like to have it, keep observing that image, and make it a part of your own reality.

PLAY NEW AGE MUSIC FOR TWO MINUTES.

That ideal body image is becoming more and more real, you are seeing it very clearly, and seeing it in its full size and dimensions. And now that you are going to step forward and into that body, you will find yourself in that body, so that you can try it out and make certain it is just the body you do want to have. And if there is something you would like to change, make those changes now. See yourself free of all desire to smoke.

Move around in that body, feel its strength and agility, its dynamic aliveness, its surging vitality, and be certain that its appearance and all of its attributes are what you realistically desire. And as you occupy that body, coming to know that body very well, your present physical body is going to be drawn into that new mold. You are moving already toward the realization of that ideal body image, and you will be doing whatever is needed to achieve that body you want to have. You are now a nonsmoker.

PLAY NEW AGE MUSIC FOR FOUR MINUTES.

End your trance as usual.

Alcoholism

Alcoholics have a compulsive personality that may be altered through the proper use of self-hypnosis. Hypnosis can facilitate their ability to adapt in an empowered manner to stress.

A Self-Hypnosis Exercise

The following exercise can be practiced to overcome excessive drinking.

From now on, you will want to give up drinking altogether. Your desire and determination to give it up will become so strong, so powerful, that it will completely overwhelm your craving to drink. You will begin to feel a strong dislike for alcohol in any form.

Every day, your craving will become less and less, weaker and weaker, until it disappears completely. You will realize, more and more, that alcohol is a poison to you. Whenever you feel that you simply must have a drink, sucking on a hard candy, which you will carry with you at all times from now on, will immediately remove the urge to drink, and you will quickly become both relaxed and comfortable. Thinking of the number 20 three times will also increase this feeling of comfort and relaxation.

You have the power to stop drinking. Just as you have the power to relax every muscle in your body, as you are doing now, so can you control any and all of your habits, including drinking.

You will stop drinking as soon as you desire. And it will be because you really want to do so down deep inside. I am only a friend who wishes to guide you as long as you need me.

With each passing day, your desire to drink is going to become less and less. With each passing day, you are going to feel stronger and stronger as a person, and your need to drink will be correspondingly decreased. With each passing day, you are going to derive more and more pleasure out of life, and so you will have less and less need to dull your senses with alcohol.

If you should ever feel a need to take a drink of alcohol, just say 20, 20, 20, and this urge will lessen and disappear. The next time you are at a party where alcoholic drinks are served, you are going to find that a soft drink will satisfy your craving just as much as one that contains alcohol. Soft drinks, by themselves, will satisfy your desire to drink completely. You will be able to enjoy yourself and have a good time at the party without consuming any alcohol whatsoever. And any time your craving should return momentarily, another soft drink will completely eliminate it once more. You will remain completely sober throughout the entire evening. And afterward, you will realize that you had a much more enjoyable time than you would have had if you had been drinking.

You are steadily losing your desire for alcohol.

You are a free and powerful being who, beginning today, will eliminate once and for all any tendency to drink alcohol. Your body and mind will heal and balance themselves. You have all the inner strength necessary to create your new reality free of alcoholic beverages.

You are in control of your life and are confident about your ability to permanently eliminate alcohol from your reality. Every day, you are programming your subconscious to accomplish this goal.

You unconditionally love and accept yourself and desire to free yourself of alcohol once and for all. You have the self-discipline to accomplish your personal and professional goals. Every day, in every way, you increase your self-discipline. You do what you need to do and stop doing what doesn't work. You now adapt, and you keep pace with the movements of change. You always consider your options, and you always act in your best interest. You are self-reliant and self-confident. You are filled with independence and determination. You project a positive self-image. You can do whatever you set your mind to.

Mentally see an image of yourself standing before you. This is your body, exactly as you would like it to appear, free of any and all desires to drink alcohol. Examine it more and more closely now, and it will be a realistic, but ideal, body image, one that you *really could achieve, and one that you will achieve. And when you have a clear image of your body as you would like to have it, keep observing that image, and make it a part of your own reality.*

PLAY NEW AGE MUSIC FOR TWO MINUTES.

That ideal body image is becoming more and more real. You are seeing it very clearly, and seeing it in its full size and dimensions. And now that you are going to step forward and into that body, you will find yourself in that body, so that you can try it out and make certain that it is just the body you do want to have. And if there is something you would like to change, make those changes now. See yourself free of all desires to drink alcohol.

Move around in that body. Feel its strength and agility, its dynamic aliveness, its surging vitality, and make really certain that its appearance and all its attributes are what you realistically desire. And as you occupy that body, coming to know that body very well, your present physical body is going to be drawn into that new mold. You are moving already toward the realization of that ideal body image, and you will be doing whatever is needed to achieve that body you want to have. You are completely free of all alcoholic tendencies.

PLAY NEW AGE MUSIC FOR FOUR MINUTES.

End your trance as usual.

Obsessive-Compulsive Disorder

People with obsessive-compulsive disorder (OCD) exhibit recurrent and persistent thoughts (obsessions) that result in stress, and engage in repetitive behaviors (compulsions) because they feel driven to perfection.

A Self-Hypnosis Exercise

Practice the following script to eliminate this self-defeating behavior:

You are a free and powerful being who, beginning today, will eliminate once and for all any obsessive-compulsive behavior.

Your body and mind will heal and balance themselves. You have all the inner strength necessary to create your new reality free of obsessive-compulsive behavior.

You are in control of your life and are confident about your ability to permanently eliminate obsessive-compulsive behavior from your reality. Every day, you are raising your soul's energy to accomplish this goal.

You unconditionally love and accept yourself and desire to free yourself of obsessive-compulsive disorder. You have the self-discipline to accomplish your personal and professional goals. Every day, in every way, you increase your self-discipline. You do what you need to do, and stop doing what doesn't work. You now adapt, and you keep pace with the movements of change. You always consider your options and always act in your best interest. You are self-reliant and self-confident. You are filled with independence and determination. You project a positive self-image. You can do whatever you set your mind to.

You see positive opportunities in everything you experience. Every day, you feel better about yourself. You are optimistic. You are enthusiastic and look forward to challenges. You detach from all negativity. Your positive self-image generates success and happiness. You are now at peace with yourself, the world, and everyone in it. You deserve the best life has to offer. You detach from pressure and retreat to a calmer inner space. You handle your responsibilities with harmonious ease. You accept the things you cannot change, and change the things you can. You are at peace with yourself.

You now have absolute faith in your subconscious and your new positive reality, free of obsessive-compulsive tendencies. All causes and factors previously associated with the obsessive-compulsive disorder are now disappearing permanently. Every day, in every way, you are getting better and better. Negative thoughts and suggestions have no influence over you at any mind level.

Mentally see an image of yourself standing before you. This is your body exactly as you would like it to appear, free of any and all obsessive-compulsive behavior. Examine it more and more closely now, and it will be a realistic, but ideal, body image, one that you really could achieve, and one that you will achieve. And when you have a very clear image of your body as you would like to have it, keep observing that image, and make it a part of your own reality.

PLAY NEW AGE MUSIC FOR TWO MINUTES.

That ideal body image is becoming more and more real. You are seeing it clearly, and in its full size and dimensions. And now that you are going to step forward into that body, you will find yourself in that body, so that you can try it out and make certain that it is just the body you do want to have. And if you would like to change something, make those changes now. See yourself free of all obsessive-compulsive behavior.

Move around in that body. Feel its strength and agility, its dynamic aliveness, its surging vitality, and make really certain that its appearance and all of its attributes are what you realistically desire. And as you occupy that body, coming to know that body very well, your present physical body is going to be drawn into that new mold. You are moving already toward the realization of that ideal body image, and you will be doing whatever is needed to achieve the body you want to have. You are completely free of all obsessive-compulsive tendencies.

PLAY NEW AGE MUSIC FOR FOUR MINUTES.

End your trance as usual.

Nail Biting

Nail biting is usually indicative of anxiety and insecurity. Although most commonly observed in children, it is exhibited by people of any age.

A Self-Hypnosis Exercise

The following script may be used to remove this unwanted behavior.

You are a very attractive person. You do not want your appearance to be spoiled by ugly hands. Nice hands and shapely nails will make you even more attractive, and you will want to make every effort to stop biting your nails and spoiling them.

You will be able to stop biting them altogether, and then they will soon begin to grow. As your nerves become stronger and steadier, as you become calmer and more relaxed each day, you will have no reason to go on biting your nails.

By using self-hypnosis, you will no longer want to bite them; you will stop biting them. If at any time you do start to bite them without realizing what you are doing, the moment your fingers touch your mouth you will know immediately what you are doing and will be able to stop yourself right away—before you have done any damage. From now on, you will stop biting your nails, they will begin to grow, and you will begin to feel proud of your hands.

You owe your body this respect and protection. You will weigh the pros and cons each time you are about to bite your nails. Associate the relaxation of your muscles that you now feel with your ability to control your habits. Do not think about nail biting. If you repeatedly deny satisfaction to an urge or desire by ignoring it, it eventually goes away.

Whenever your hand starts to move toward your mouth for the purpose of biting your nails, you will become aware of it before it reaches your mouth. You will then say to yourself, or aloud, Do I really want to bite my nails? If your answer is yes, go ahead and enjoy it! But chances are, when you are aware of doing something so foolish, you'd rather not, so you won't. You are in complete control of all your habits. If the desire to bite your nails arises, you will say to yourself, I no longer bite my nails, and I don't need to, then think of how healthy your nails look. You are steadily losing your desire to bite your nails.

Grinding Teeth

Bruxism is the term applied to the clenching or grinding of teeth. The habit eventually reduces the height of the teeth and makes them more susceptible to cavities.

A Self-Hypnosis Exercise

Use the following script to eliminate bruxism.

Whenever you grind your teeth or tighten your cheek muscles, you will want to keep your mouth slightly open, wide enough to place your tongue between your back teeth. This will help your muscles to become loose. This will stop your muscles from cramping. The longer your tongue stays between your teeth, the more your muscles will become loose and limp, like wet cotton.

From now on, as you continue your relaxation into sleep, let your mind dwell on the phrase, "Lips together, teeth apart." In addition, when you feel the need to grind or clench your teeth, clench your fists instead.

Gaining Weight

Some people simply don't eat enough food and end up below the desired weight for their height and bone structure. This is an unhealthy situation that can compromise their overall health.

A Self-Hypnosis Exercise

Add additional weight and overcome poor eating habits.

Being underweight is unhealthy. You need your body to live. You owe your body this respect and protection.

You have the power to reprogram your subconscious to reverse previous thoughts of undereating and thinking of yourself as being underweight. You will, starting today, reprogram your subconscious to think of yourself as weighing your ideal weight of _____ and eating only those foods that are healthy for your body.

You are going to gain all the weight that you desire until you reach your ideal weight of _____ and you are going to do this starting today. I want you to see yourself as you desire to be. See yourself at your ideal weight of _____. You have the power to create your own reality. See yourself as weighing your ideal weight, and you will reach this weight.

See others around you admiring your new weight and complimenting you on how good you look. This is your reality, and starting today your subconscious mind will begin making this reality come true.

I want you to associate this relaxed state that you are in right now with a relaxed attitude about gaining weight. After you finish a meal you will still be hungry. You will eat larger portions of foods that are healthy and necessary for your body.

I want you to say to yourself, "I am gaining weight steadily every day." Right now, I want you to set a realistic goal for gaining weight. Decide right now how many pounds you can realistically gain each week, and you will gain this exact amount. Now, repeat to yourself the realistic amount of weight you can gain each week to reach your ideal weight of _____.

You are steadily losing your desire to be underweight.

End trance as usual.

Goals

Long-term goals refer to major things we wish to accomplish eventually in our lives. Short-term goals refer to things we must do more or less immediately. Long-term goals are generally achieved by accomplishing many short-term goals.

- Decide if the goal is an appropriate one for you. It helps to talk to others and learn from their experiences. In this end, you will have to make the decision.
- Make your long-term goals general, rather than specific. If they are too specific, you are inviting failure.

- Once a long-term goal has been selected, analyze it in terms of the short-term goals that must be achieved to get there. Determine what path your short-term goals should take. There is almost always more than one way to achieve a long-term goal.

- Start now. Begin working systematically on the short-term goals. Most people underestimate the length of time it will take to accomplish a goal. Be patient with your goals.

Short-term goals are easier to achieve when these rules are followed:

- They should be realistic. They should be small, discrete steps leading toward the long-term goal.

- They should be more specific than long-term goals.

- Your approach should be organized and planned in such a way that you have a high probability of accomplishment.

- If you fail at one of your short-term goals, do not magnify it out of proportion. Simply figure out an alternate route that will get you around the obstacle.

- When you achieve a short-term goal, reward yourself.

Once the long-term and short-term goals have been established, program them into the subconscious using your rules for formulating autosuggestions. After this has been accomplished, do not concentrate on your goals. Goals are for direction and planning. After they have been formulated, you need to put them in the back of your mind and begin to concentrate on the present. With a properly programmed subconscious, you carry out your goals much better than you could ever hope to do consciously.

Final Thoughts

Eliminating bad habits should not be rushed. You probably have exhibited these unwanted habits for several years. These self-hypnosis scripts can be repeated as often as necessary.

The more seriously self-hypnosis is taken, the more rapid the results. Yet taking it seriously does not mean straining toward it. That would prevent relaxation, which is the first requirement.

After self-hypnosis is reached, allow time for the suggestion to become seeded in the subconscious mind (so it can then be acted upon). This occurs more rapidly with some suggestions than with others.

Once the suggestion has been planted in the subconscious, from that time on, only occasional reinforcements will be necessary. The new habit will have become ingrained and automatic. Research has demonstrated that it requires 21 days for a new habit to be accepted by the mind. In case temptations do arise from time to time, just repeat the self-hypnosis exercises to ensure long-lasting success.

CHAPTER 3

HYPNOTIZE YOUR
PHOBIAS AWAY

We are all exposed to events in our lives that are frightening and cause us to avoid a repeat of those circumstances. If the emotional discomfort is rationally based, it is simply classified as a fear. An irrational fear of something is labeled as a phobia.

Common phobias are:

- Claustrophobia is a fear of confined places.
- Hydrophobia is a fear of water.
- Acrophobia is a fear of heights.
- Agoraphobia a fear of open spaces.

Phobias are not the result of biochemical or genetic factors, but are behaviors learned from past experiences. Phobias may be acquired by mimicking parents, teachers, or other role models. These irrational fears may originate at any age, and are easily eliminated through the use of hypnosis.

To exhibit a phobia, an individual must be under severe stress; however, stress is a matter of interpretation. What is stressful to one person may not be to another. How do you know if you are under stress? Consider these signs of stress (if you possess seven or more of these, you are most likely overstressed):

- Frequent, nervous eye blinking.
- Easily irritated.
- The lack of a sense of humor.
- Digestive problems.
- Regular sensations of tenseness.
- Insomnia.
- Too much sleep (hypersomnia).
- Cold hands.
- Nervous habits such as frequent tapping of fingers.
- Clenching of the jaw and grinding of the teeth.
- Shallow and irregular breathing.
- Frequent tension headaches.
- Feelings of inadequacy.
- Hyperactivity, such as moving legs back and forth rapidly when seated.
- Extreme increase or decrease in appetite.
- Clouded thoughts and difficulty in thinking.
- Obsessive thoughts and compulsive behavior.

The methods presented in this chapter will assist you in dealing with stress. Here are some approaches you will find helpful in overcoming stress.

- Establish a priority for daily activities. Keep an active list, and complete tasks in order of importance.
- Always be yourself. Do not try to please anyone.
- Develop a realistic attitude toward accomplishing goals. Some things may have to wait until the next day.
- Select restful hobbies and physical activities that allow you to relax. Constant involvement in competitive sports only adds more stress.
- Be optimistic at all times. Be especially positive about the future.
- Master relaxation exercises.
- Eliminate the tendency to be a perfectionist. Nobody is perfect (notice that all pencils come with erasers).

+ Be assertive and confront people who upset you. Don't accumulate hurt feelings.
+ Learn from your mistakes without dwelling on them. Perceive all setbacks as learning opportunities and challenges to be overcome.
+ Incorporate breaks in your day, and practice relaxation exercises.
+ Discuss your problems, anxieties, and fears with family and friends.
+ Recall only positive past events.
+ Use low-key exercises to work off tension and frustration.
+ Refrain from insisting you're always right.
+ Always deal with the basic causes of stress rather than the symptoms.

Building Your Self-Image

Now that some of the basic mind-body techniques for dealing with stress have been discussed, the next step is to train yourself to build up your self-image. By changing any negative attitudes and lower self-confidence levels to positive, higher ones, the tendency to become discouraged or depressed about your life is eliminated. This functions to ensure your ultimate success and eliminate the tendency to develop phobias.

You absolutely must develop feelings of self-esteem and confidence to become empowered. No amount of willpower can surmount the feeling of defeatism. Any negative thoughts will filter into your subconscious mind, which does not question or analyze the data it receives. If you have experienced repeated failure in past attempts to change a behavior pattern, your total self-image becomes established and fixed as one of failure. You become so convinced that you are incapable of reversing this trend that you eventually stop picturing a desirable goal for yourself. You resign yourself to accepting the current situation as being permanent and helpless.

A positive self-image must be fed into your subconscious mind without being evaluated by the critical factor of your conscious mind proper (defense mechanisms). The most efficient and effective method of accomplishing this goal is by practicing self-hypnosis.

Although many obstacles may arise during your consciousness-raising program, the proper use of self-programming will transform these former roadblocks into stepping-stones of success. Once you envision succeeding in your goals, former difficulties disappear, and the subconscious becomes your chief ally in strengthening your ability to meet challenges.

The subconscious mind contains all memories. It is a natural computer and is continually being programmed with data originating from the conscious mind proper. The subconscious cannot alter this data; however, it does direct the conscious mind to act in a specific way. The conscious mind is always resistant to change, any change, even if it is for the better. The conscious mind likes business as usual. Consciousness raising and behavioral changes are not business as usual; therefore, the conscious mind is your only enemy.

By seeing yourself as you desire to be, you are reprogramming your subconscious computer. This does not require a critical acceptance, because your subconscious is incapable of analytical thought. Accompanying this visualization will be a feeling that you have already attained this goal. This as-if approach is remarkably successful.

Once you achieve a particular goal using the subconscious mind, the maintenance of this goal will be effortless. When something attempts to interfere with the proper functioning of the reprogrammed subconscious, your internal computer will recognize the error immediately, and it will be corrected by this feedback mechanism.

Your initial efforts in reprogramming the subconscious require a certain amount of mental training, which encompasses all new goals and aspirations. Daily practice of the exercises presented in this book results in a permanent reprogramming of the subconscious computer and a spontaneous incorporation of this goal. Willpower is neither necessary nor desirable for this paradigm. This is one example of raising consciousness.

Your imagination can create a new mental image of yourself. If you have properly implanted the subconscious with positive images and suggestions, you automatically alter your behavior to act in accordance with this new programming. A new sense of well-being and accomplishment accompany this pattern of behavior. You will be able to feel this sense of confidence and empowerment for prolonged periods following additional practice sessions.

Willpower alone cannot result in permanent changes in behavior. If it could, you would not be reading this book. The problem with the willpower approach is that you are consciously placing too much emphasis on past failures. As a result, your mental mind-set is not conducive to improvement, and subsequent efforts prove only more frustrating.

Success in applying consciousness-raising techniques depends on the subconscious mind's uncritical acceptance of constructive suggestions. I have found the most effective method of achieving this is through the use of self-hypnosis.

A Self-Hypnosis Exercise

This exercise is on track 2 of the CD in the back of this book.

Use the following simple self-hypnosis script to boost your self-image:

Relaxation through self-hypnosis will allow you to generate a feeling of inner tranquility and peace of mind. You will now be able to deal with everyday life in an empowered manner. Although you may not be able to change your environment, you will be able to adjust yourself to it and deal positively with the persons, places, or things that formerly created stress.

Whatever your mind can create, you can easily achieve. Each and every time you give yourself positive suggestions, your subconscious mind will accept them and reprogram out previous negative behaviors or self-images.

You are a free and powerful being who, beginning today, will eliminate once and for all any negative behaviors or beliefs. Your body and mind will heal and balance themselves. You have all the inner strength necessary to create your new reality of an empowered and assertive human being.

You unconditionally love and accept yourself and possess the self-discipline to accomplish your personal and professional goals. Every day, in every way, you increase your self-discipline. You do what you need to do and stop doing what doesn't work. You now adapt, and you keep pace with the movements of change. You always consider your options, and you always act in your own best interest. You are self-reliant and self-confident. You are filled with independence and determination. You project a positive self-image. You can do whatever you set your mind to.

You are persistent, determined, and ambitious. You complete each task because you are a success-oriented winner. You fulfill each personal and professional desire in a relentless, efficient, and empowered manner.

You have the self-discipline to accomplish all your personal and professional goals. Each day that passes will result in an increase in your self-discipline. You can now complete large and complicated tasks by breaking them down into smaller components and doing each job one step at a time.

You are clear and focused on your values and have no reservations about committing to your goals. You remain alert and focused on what you are doing. You can routinely block out all thoughts except those related to what you are doing. You are a winner and will now always exhibit a success-type personality. You are self-reliant and self-confident.

You are filled with independence and determination. You are at peace with yourself and the universe. You do things that make you proud of yourself. You feel safe, secure, and protected. Every day, in every manner, you are more confident in your ability to handle anything that comes your way.

Hierarchies

Because phobias are learned responses, these anxiety reactions can be eliminated by purposely creating opposing responses to the ones associated with the phobia. Through self-hypnosis, you simply give yourself instructions to become exposed gradually to situations, people, or objects that previously evoked a phobic response and suggest relaxation to replace the previous anxiety-filled association.

Constructing a hierarchy is the simplest method of accomplishing this task. By visualizing an item from the lower end (less stressful) of the hierarchy and using relaxation to counter its emotional effect, the phobic association eventually disappears after repeated trials. This process continues as you move to more anxiety-laden items on your list, until all stimuli have been desensitized.

For example, the following hierarchy was constructed by a patient with a fear of flying:

1. Turbulence.
2. A light-headed feeling from the plane's motion.
3. The pilot announces a delay in landing.
4. Looking at my watch and noticing we should have landed by this time.
5. The "fasten seat belt" sign goes on at an unexpected time.
6. Reduction or changes in engine sounds.
7. Overhearing a passenger talk about an airliner crash.
8. Changes in the cabin lighting.
9. Feeling of being pushed back in seat as the plane goes down the runway for takeoff.
10. The first part of the takeoff when I look outside.
11. Taxiing for takeoff.
12. Boarding the aircraft.
13. Standing in line to check bags.
14. Buying the tickets in advance.
15. The morning of the trip.
16. The night before the trip.
17. Two days before the trip.
18. Five days before the trip.
19. A week before the trip.
20. At home or in the office, realizing this is it—the trip by plane can't be avoided.
21. Watching an airplane take off on television.

Because the least stressful scenes are at the bottom of the hierarchy, the patient works in reverse sequence. After entering a relaxed state, the patient then introduces the first imagery scene from the bottom of the hierarchy.

A Self-Hypnosis Exercise

This exercise is on track 3 of the CD in the back of this book.

The following exercise constructs a hierarchy that can be used to overcome phobias:

> *As you continue to relax, automatically going deeper and deeper, picture yourself relaxing at home in your favorite chair, watching TV, relaxing more and more all the time. You're watching a TV program in which an airplane is taking off.*
>
> *(Pause for three seconds.)*
>
> *Just switch off that image now and go back to relaxing.*

Once the anxiety response to a specific item at the bottom of the hierarchy is eliminated, the patient moves up the list to the next one.

A Sample Hierarchy

The following is an example of the flying phobia hierarchy:

> *As you continue to relax, you find you can relax more and more. You notice that you are becoming less anxious, and more relaxed, with each scene. Imagine it's one week before the trip when you must fly in an airplane; picture that in your mind. Now switch off that scene, allowing yourself to become more and more relaxed all over. You can relax more and more on your own, enjoying the ability to control your own level of relaxation. Good. That's fine. Realizing more and more how easy it is to feel calm and serene. The next time I give you the scene, just as in real life, your anxiety level will be much, much lower; you will be able to relax throughout the visualization. Once again, just imagine it's one week before you must fly in an airplane.*

This represents a simple method of systematically desensitizing an anxiety response from a potential stressor.

Dental Phobia Hierarchy

For a dental phobia, one of my patients prepared the following hierarchy and began with item number 21, and worked backward to item number one.

1. Having a tooth removed.
2. Having a root canal performed.
3. Having a dental impression taken.
4. Having dental instruments manipulated in my mouth.
5. Having a tooth drilled.
6. Receiving the anesthesia injection.
7. Seeing the needles and syringe.
8. Having a probe placed in a cavity.
9. Seeing the dental instruments.
10. Hearing the noise of the drill.
11. The dentist telling me that I have many dental problems.
12. Having the dentist squirt air and water in my mouth.
13. Having my teeth cleaned.
14. Having dental X rays taken.
15. The dentist walks into the treatment room.
16. Reclining in a dental chair.
17. Sitting up in a dental chair.
18. Smelling the odors of a dentist's office.
19. Sitting in the dentist's waiting room.
20. Calling to make a dental appointment.
21. Thinking about going to the dentist.

Overcoming dental phobias is easier than you may have previously thought. I used techniques such as this for 13 years in my dental practice to assist my patients in ridding themselves of these irrational fears.

A Sample Hierarchy

The following technique, a modified hierarchy approach, can be used to combat any phobia.

As you continue to relax, automatically going deeper and deeper, picture yourself relaxing at home in your favorite chair, watching TV, or listening to music. Now I want you to picture yourself, as best as you can, in the most relaxing environment you have ever experienced. Keep this image as a reference point and go back to it when I say relax.

Perceive yourself being exposed to what you fear, but to a very small degree. This scene represents the weakest association with your phobia. Do this now. Relax and think of the pleasant scene you created earlier.

Now, see yourself being placed in the phobic situation to a greater degree. Do this now with complete confidence. Relax and see how much control your mind has over your body.

Continue with four to six additional advanced phobic scenes.

Relax once more. Now, you will be able to apply this technique in real life. The next time you are exposed to the phobic environment, your anxiety level will be much lower, and you will be able to relax by using this simple exercise. Each time you are exposed to what you now fear, your fearful response will decrease (until soon it disappears completely).

A Self-Hypnosis Exercise

The following exercise can be practiced to eliminate a fear of dentists.

Your muscles are tight rubber bands that are progressively unwinding and becoming looser and looser. This will continue until you feel that every bit of tension is gone, or until the muscles are as loose and relaxed as you want them to be today. This wonderful relaxation will be such a help to you that you will be very comfortable during your next dental appointment. At future appointments, you will notice the unwinding of all the muscles in your body beginning as soon as you enter the office.

When you are seated in the dental chair, you will say to yourself 20, 20, 20 and immediately feel the relaxation developing. The dental chair will feel very soft and comfortable and will remind you of your favorite resting chair at home.

Concentrate on enjoying this wonderful, relaxing feeling. The various sounds and noises that you hear will have the same soothing effect as listening to your favorite music. Your fears of a dental appointment will cease to exist. You will be able to allow the necessary dental treatment to be carried out. You will experience no fear whatsoever during the entire time you spend with the dentist. You will experience no fear whatsoever during appointments in which teeth need to be removed, filled, and so on. You are steadily losing your vulnerability to be afraid of a dentist or dental procedures.

Overcoming dental fears empowers individuals and raises their self-image.

Gagging

Try this script to eliminate an exaggerated gag reflex.

Before all dental procedures, you will be relaxed, calm, and comfortable, and you will experience only a normal gag reflex. The excessive gag reflex will be eliminated and you will remain relaxed, calm, and comfortable during dental procedures.

Dental Office Visit

The next section details a more complex script that can once and for all eliminate long-standing fears of dentistry.

A Self-Hypnosis Exercise

The following is a proven approach for dealing with a fear of dentists.

As I talk to you for a moment about something you already know a lot about...remembering and forgetting...you know a lot about it, because we all do a lot of it...every moment of every day you remember...and then you forget, so you can remember something else...you can't remember everything all at once, so you let some memories move quietly back in your mind...I wonder, for example, whether you remember what you had for lunch yesterday...I would guess that, with not too much effort, you can remember what you had for lunch yesterday...and yet...I wonder if you remember what you had for lunch a month ago today...I would guess the effort is really too great to dig up that memory, although of course it is there...somewhere, deep in the back of your mind.

There is no need to remember, so you don't...and I wonder whether you'll be pleased to notice that the things we talk about today, with your eyes closed, are things that you'll remember tomorrow or the next day...or next week...I wonder if you'll decide to let the memory of these rest quietly in the back of your mind...or whether you'll remember gradually, a bit at a time...or perhaps all at once, to be again resting in the back of your mind.

Perhaps you'll be surprised to notice that the reception room is the place for memory to surface...perhaps not...perhaps you'll notice that it is more comfortable to remember on another day altogether...it really doesn't matter...doesn't matter at all. Whatever you do, or choose to remember, however, is just fine...absolutely natural...doesn't matter at all...whether you remember tomorrow or the next day, whether you remember it at once, or gradually...completely, or only partially...whether you let the memory rest quietly and comfortably in the back of your mind...really doesn't matter at all. And I wonder whether you'll notice that you'll feel surprised that your visit here today is so much more pleasant and comfortable than you might have expected...I wonder whether you'll notice that surprise...that there are no other feelings...perhaps you'll feel curious about that surprise...surprise, curiosity.

I wonder whether you'll be pleased to notice that today...and any day...whenever you feel your head resting back against a dental chair...when you feel your head resting back like this...you'll feel reminded of how very comfortable you are feeling right now... even more comfortable than you feel even now...comfortable, relaxed...nothing to bother, nothing to disturb. I wonder whether you'll be reminded of this comfort, too, and relaxation, just by noticing the brightness of the light on the ceiling...perhaps this comfort and relaxation will come flooding back, quickly and automatically, whenever you find yourself beginning to sit down in the dental chair. I don't know exactly how it will seem...I only know, as perhaps you also know...that your experience will seem surprisingly more pleasant, surprisingly more comfortable, surprisingly more restful than you might expect...with nothing to bother, nothing to disturb...whatever you are able to notice...everything can be a part of your experience of comfortableness, restfulness, and relaxation...everything you notice can be a part of being absolutely comfortable.

And I want to remind you that whenever you say "20, 20, 20" whenever it is appropriate, and only when it is appropriate...whenever you say "20, 20, 20" to yourself...a feeling...a feeling of being ready to do something...perhaps a feeling of being ready to close your eyes...perhaps a feeling of being ready to be even more comfortable...perhaps ready to know even more clearly that there's nothing to bother, nothing to disturb...perhaps ready to become heavy and tired...I don't know...but whenever you say "20, 20, 20" you'll experience a feeling...a feeling of being ready to do something. It really doesn't matter...perhaps just a feeling of being ready to be even more surprised...it doesn't really matter...relaxation...absolute deep comfort and relaxation... with nothing to bother and nothing to disturb...that's fine...and now, as you continue to enjoy your comfortable relaxation, I'd like you to notice how very nice it feels to be this way...to really enjoy your own experience, to really enjoy the feelings your body can give you.

You can now use this training to be relaxed during your next visit to the dentist.

A Phobia-Elimination Visual-Imagery Exercise

The following visualization script can be used to eliminate any phobia.

You are a free and powerful being who, beginning today, will eliminate once and for all any phobias from your awareness. Your body and mind will heal and balance itself. You have all the inner strength necessary to create your new reality free of phobias.

You are in control of your life and are confident about your ability to permanently eliminate phobias from your reality. Every day, you are reprogramming your subconscious to accomplish this goal.

You unconditionally love and accept yourself, and deserve to free yourself of phobias. You have the self-discipline to accomplish your personal and professional goals. Every day, in every way, you increase your self-discipline. You do what you need to do, and stop doing what doesn't work. You now adapt, and you keep pace with the movements of change. You always consider your options, and you always act in your best interest. You are self-reliant and self-confident. You are filled with independence and determination. You project a very positive self-image. You can do whatever you set your mind to.

Mentally picture an image of yourself standing before you. This is your body exactly as you would like it to appear, free of any and all phobias. Examine it more and more closely now, and it will be a realistic, but ideal, body image, one that you really could achieve, and one that you will achieve. And when you have a very clear image of your body as you would like to have it, keep observing that image, and make it a part of your own reality.

PLAY NEW AGE MUSIC FOR TWO MINUTES.

That ideal body image is becoming more and more real. You are seeing it very clearly, and seeing it in its full size and dimensions. And now that you are going to step forward into that body, you will find yourself in that body so that you can try it out and make certain that it is just the body you do want to have. And if there is something you would like to change, make those changes now. See yourself free of all phobias.

Move around in that body; feel its strength and agility, its dynamic aliveness, its surging vitality, and make really certain that its appearance and all of its attributes are what you realistically desire. And as you occupy that body, coming to know that body very well, your present physical body is going to be drawn into that new mold. You are already moving toward the realization of that ideal body image, and you will be doing whatever is needed to achieve that body you want to have. You are completely free of all phobic tendencies.

PLAY NEW AGE MUSIC FOR FOUR MINUTES.

End your trance as usual.

Final Thoughts

To permanently change beliefs, individuals must move beyond positive thinking alone. This can be accomplished only by reprogramming the subconscious. This is why self-hypnosis is so successful when used properly. The subconscious—not the ego—is responsible for creating reality. By applying the simple methods presented in this chapter, any phobia can be permanently eliminated.

CHAPTER 4

SLOW DOWN
THE AGING PROCESS

Taking control of the physical body is part of empowerment. Slowing down the aging process is quite possible, as will be discussed in this chapter. In certain instances, the process of aging can even be reversed!

We, as a society, are striving not just to live longer, but to live better. We seek a way to avoid the chronic diseases, encroaching fatigue, and degrading changes that seem to characterize old age. As a nation, we are searching to find what we can do to make our lives better, extend our most healthy, vibrant, active years, and shorten the time of weakness and failing health. We are a people ripe and ready to empower ourselves and apply natural youthing techniques.

Science has made great strides in the understanding of just what aging is, how it works, and—most important of all—what we can do about it. We can reduce the diseases of aging and prolong our health and vital years. In short, we are now able to look younger and live longer naturally.

More than 85 percent of the debilitating illnesses of old age result from only a handful of diseases—cancer, coronary artery disease, stroke, diabetes, kidney failure, obstructive lung disease, pneumonia, and influenza. Heart disease, all by itself, accounts for one out of every two deaths of older Americans, and high blood pressure directly causes or contributes to 15 percent of all deaths. We now can control even these pathologies by our lifestyle.

The most important message of this chapter is to keep a young mind and healthy body. Enthusiasm, meeting people, having plans, and keeping busy is what I mean by a young mind. Many older people simply give up and decide that their lives are over. I suggest you look to the future, a long future.

Living in the past is a sign of depression. Old memories are fine, but you've still got time to make new memories. When people get a little older they are frightened to make a change in their lives. It's easier to stay in that same, safe rut. To me, that challenge is what keeps us alive and "in the flow."

Just because you're chronologically old doesn't mean you can't lead a full, vigorous, and active life. Open your mind to it. Don't just sit there—do things. The possibilities are endless. Try doing something nice for somebody who doesn't expect it. You'll be surprised by how good you'll feel.

Certain behavioral characteristics surface when a person lives in fear of growing older. Some of these are:

- Imitating younger people. Adopting the mannerisms and dress of much younger individuals only invites ridicule from those around you.
- Apologizing for reaching a certain age. Instead of expressing appreciation for having attained an age of understanding and wisdom, some people make apologies for turning 40, 50, or older.
- Exhibiting a premature slowdown and developing an inferiority complex as a result of advancing age.
- Spending excessive amounts of time worrying about dying. This is more prevalent with people who lack purpose in their lives.
- Developing an actual fear of death. This usually coincides with an assumption of physical and mental degeneration of aging, or an eventual end of all consciousness with death.
- Associating old age with poverty.

What were once accepted as inevitable difficulties associated with aging have been shown by science to be preventable, or at least delayed.

Problems and worries such as high blood pressure, wrinkles, weight problems, aches and pains, heart problems, and cancer can be prevented with proper lifestyle adjustment. The result is a longer and more fulfilling life.

I like to call living an extended and quality life "well-span," rather than "life span." Living the longest possible life, and being energetic, fully alert, and radiantly alive is definitely within grasp.

I refer to the slowing down of the aging process as "youthing." "Youthing" is one way to enjoy a longer and more fulfilled life, while raising your consciousness at the same time. The human body is designed to live to at least 120, some say 140, years. Today, Americans live, on average, only 75 years. With proper training, and by following nature's intent, however, it is not difficult to see how we can add 45 to 65 years to our lives. My estimate of 25 to 50 years is a rather conservative one at that!

To incorporate this "youthing" process in your well-span requires approximately 20 minutes each day for exercise and self-hypnosis. Is that a lot to ask for qualitatively extending your life by 25 to 50 years?

No drugs, surgery, or artificial elements of any kind are presented in my "youthing" approach. In some cases, the aging process can actually be reversed. By following these recommendations and simple techniques, I can assure you of a longer and happier life. Ignoring these suggestions will unquestionably result in a shortened, less healthy, and far less productive life.

When it comes to "youthing," it is clear that the most significant differences lie in the choices we make many times each day—that is, decisions about what we eat, how we move, how we treat ourselves, even what inner tapes we play as we drift to sleep at night. If you are age 50 or so, you can expect to add 25 to 50 quality years to your life with this program. Those of you under 30 could see this figure swell to 45 to 65 quality years.

- ◆ It is the immune system that is the key to slowing down the aging process. It is one of the first bodily systems to deteriorate with advancing age. Consider the following examples of what happens to the human body as the immune system deteriorates: Most classic diseases of aging, such as heart disease, arthritis, cancer, and pneumonia, occur only after the immune system begins to lose its potency.

- ♦ When the aging immune system loses its efficiency in cleansing the body of defective and dead normal cells, this buildup of cellular garbage facilitates the aging of other organs.
- ♦ The immune system begins to attack the body itself (through autoimmune diseases such as arthritis), upon aging.
- ♦ Scientists believe that the same genes that guide the aging process control the immune system.

What is important to understand throughout this discussion of the immune system is that the use of self-hypnosis increases the production of the hormone dehydroepiandrosterone (DHEA) by the adrenal cortex. DHEA has been shown to increase the immune system's response to most of the diseases commonly associated with aging.

Many people today have heard the media hype on a hormone supplement known as DHEA. The problem with taking any supplements is the side effects. Some of the side effects associated with DHEA are:

- ♦ Acne.
- ♦ Oily skin.
- ♦ Facial hair growth on women.
- ♦ Deepening of the voice.
- ♦ Irritability.
- ♦ Insomnia.
- ♦ Fatigue.
- ♦ Breast enlargement in men.
- ♦ Exacerbation of breast cancer in women and prostate cancer in men.

Throughout my career as a hypnotherapist, I have emphasized natural approaches to healing. I most definitely don't recommend DHEA supplements, so how can we increase the body's natural DHEA production and slow down aging? The answer is to practice self-hypnosis.

The adrenal glands and gonads naturally synthesize DHEA from cholesterol. The optimal levels of this hormone occur at around age 20 for women and age 25 for men. DHEA levels then gradually decline, so that by the time we reach 80, we produce less than 20 percent of the DHEA we synthesized when we were 20. This is due to stress and the decreased efficiency of our adrenal glands and gonads to convert cholesterol to DHEA.

DHEA is converted into sex hormones—estrogen for women, and testosterone in men. DHEA production is vital to our health. It functions as an antioxidant and hormone regulator. Studies have demonstrated that low levels of DHEA are associated with obesity, AIDS, cancer, diabetes, heart disease, Alzheimer's, multiple sclerosis, and compromised immune systems.

Because stress and negative emotional reactions have been linked to suppressed DHEA levels, relaxation techniques such as hypnosis are one practicable solution to this problem. Hypnosis increases the efficiency of the adrenals and gonads to produce DHEA from cholesterol. When patients practice relaxation techniques for several years, they seem to appear and act younger than their chronological age. Whether it is because of hypnosis, meditation, yoga, guided imagery, and so forth, they simply do not look their age. When patients meet me in person they are astounded at my appearance. Most say I look 15 years younger than my chronological age. (I have been using self-hypnosis informally since my college years, and formally since 1974.)

In 1975, I worked with a 32-year-old female chiropractor from the East Coast. Early in 1995, she visited my Los Angeles office with her best friend, whom she had referred to me. My former patient looked perhaps five-years older than my last mental image of her. (The chiropractor had been practicing self-hypnosis for 20 years.)

You may be wondering about what effect finding cures for diseases would have on longevity. The benefits gained from simply overcoming diseases are limited. Curing all forms of cancer, for example, would only boost the average life span by two years in the United States. If all human diseases were eliminated from the planet, in addition to all wars and accidents, the average life span would only be increased by an additional 10 to 15 years!

Hypnosis shares many commonalities with other altered states of consciousness, such as transcendental meditation (TM), yoga, and so forth, and is identical to them neurophysiologically. Keith Wallace, in 1982, conducted studies using TM to measure its effect on biological age. Individuals older than 55 who practiced TM had a younger biological age than a control population on a standardized index, which estimates biological age using blood pressure, auditory threshold, and near-point vision.[1]

Biological age shows how well a person's body is functioning in comparison to the norms of the whole population, thus giving a truer measure of how the aging process is progressing than chronological age. Some of Wallace's female subjects appeared 20 years younger than their chronological age. The longer the subjects had meditated, the younger they appeared to be.

The dividing line was between those who had meditated fewer than five years and those who had meditated five years or more. On the biological index, the group that had meditated for fewer than five years looked, on average, five years younger than their chronological age, whereas the group that had meditated for more than five years looked, on average, 12 years younger. A later study conducted in England calculated that each year of regular meditation reduces roughly one year of aging.

A recent study of 2,000 TM practitioners who subscribed to a major health insurance carrier found reduced medical utilization rates for 16 out of 17 major medical treatment categories. TM practitioners may have lower morbidity.[2] These subjects showed a marked reduction in cigarette and alcohol consumption, lowered blood pressure, and a significant improvement in autonomic and sensory processes characteristic of individuals at a much younger age.

DHEA appears to be the key to how hypnosis and other relaxation techniques retard the aging process. Many studies have shown a direct relationship between blood levels of DHEA and the inhibition of many diseases.

If you have high levels of DHEA, you are far less likely to:

- Develop arteriosclerosis and suffer from other forms of cardiovascular disease.
- Develop malignant tumors that may lead to metastatic forms of cancer.
- Lose insulin sensitivity and develop type 2 diabetes.
- Suffer a decline in mental function and lapse into dementia, Alzheimer's, or Parkinson's.

Because the previously mentioned disease states are the principal benchmarks of aging, DHEA may be the best biomarker of aging and longevity. Other conditions for which DHEA may be beneficial include autoimmune diseases, osteoporosis, Epstein-Barr viral infections, bacterial infections, memory loss and learning disabilities, chronic fatigue syndrome, AIDS (because of its immune impact), menopause, emotional instability, depression, stress, herpes 2 infections, and more.

Through the use of a simple, self-hypnotic exercise, I have trained many of my patients to slow down their aging process naturally. I personally look and feel 15 years younger than my chronological age as a result of this natural and easy-to-use 20-minute exercise that will be presented in a subsequent section of this chapter.

You are as young as you think you are. Your mind is the most powerful weapon in your arsenal against premature aging. The science of psychoneuroimmunology (PNI) studies the mind-body relationship. This multidisciplinary field relates the effects of emotions, beliefs, and attitudes on the physical body. Studies within this field have found that:

- Animals given control of their environment fight off tumors better and live longer than animals with no control.
- Patients who are programmed to expect a slow recovery after surgery exhibit more physical problems than those who expect to leave the hospital quickly, according to research conducted at Case Western Reserve University by J.K. Kiecolt-Glaser.
- Grieving, stress, and depression have all been proved to dramatically lower the body's immunological fighter cells.
- The immune system's strength reflects emotional and mental coping mechanisms. Lifestyle and psychological stresses can weaken immune defenses, increase the likelihood of catching infections, and raise the risk for many kinds of diseases.
- Patients can use mental imagery to change the levels of certain immune cells necessary to fight cancer, according to research conducted by Kiecolt-Glaser.

- People who are institutionalized, but who have some control of their lives, show dramatic improvements in overall health, and are even capable of reversing bodily changes due to aging.
- By programming themselves with mental-relaxation tools, people can lower blood pressure and reduce the frequency of heart-rhythm abnormalities.
- Brain chemicals that regulate happiness, sex drive, mental functioning, sleep, depression, aggression, and all other brain functions, have been found to activate specific immune fighters, such as scavenger cells, T-cells, antibody-producing cells, and such immune boosters as interferon and interleukin-2.

The following is a list of some lifestyle changes that can be made to facilitate longevity.

- Learn to use relaxation exercises instead of alcohol or drugs to unwind before sleep.
- Don't bring work home at night.
- Take up a hobby you enjoy.
- Create a place to relax or be by yourself, either at home or nearby.
- Learn and use time-management techniques in your daily life.
- Stop smoking.
- Make sure you get exercise every few days—30 minutes of brisk walking every other day is all you need to stay young.
- Learn to eat nutritionally balanced and wholesome meals, and include zinc-rich foods (such as liver, nuts, cheese, meat, eggs, and seafood), fruits, raw vegetables, and whole grains in your diet.
- Cut down on sweets and processed foods.
- Take time each week to do something special just for yourself.
- Join a group that gets you out with friends regularly.
- Work to bring yourself within five pounds of your ideal weight.
- Practice some form of deep relaxation (hypnosis, meditation, yoga, and so forth) on a daily basis.

Psychological factors are used by gerontologists to predict longevity. First, consider some of the circumstances that accelerate aging and shorten life span.

- Excessive worry.
- Job dissatisfaction.
- Regret for sacrifices made in the past.
- Depression.
- Lack of regular work routine.
- Financial burdens.
- Getting angry easily, or being unable to express anger.
- Criticism of self and others.
- Having to work more than 40 hours per week.
- Feeling helpless to change oneself and others.
- Loneliness, absence of close friends.
- Living alone.

Contrast those circumstances with the following factors that help extend longevity and slow down the aging process.

- Regular work routine.
- Feeling financially secure, and living within means.
- Job satisfaction.
- Happy marriage.
- Ability to laugh easily.
- Optimistic about the future.
- Regular daily routine.
- Taking at least one week's vacation every year.
- Feeling in control of personal life.
- Feeling of personal happiness.
- Ability to express feelings easily.
- Satisfactory sex life.
- Ability to make and keep close friends.
- Enjoyable leisure time, and satisfying hobbies.

From these various psychosocial factors, the most significant ones appear to be having a regular work schedule and daily routine. The younger you are when you incorporate the principles and techniques presented in this chapter, the greater the benefit.

National Institute on Aging researcher Richard Greulich coined the term "supernormals" to describe people who live beyond 100, and who are healthy and active. He noted the following common traits among these individuals.

- Their attitude toward leisure activities, security, health, and friendships are the same as those of younger people.
- They have strong feelings about being useful.
- They tend to be well educated, or come form high-level, high-responsibility jobs.
- They tend to be extroverted and remain socially active.

Greulich noted an empowerment characteristic of these supernormals. They started out mentally active, often attained a high level of formal education, and often took on high-powered jobs. After retirement, they remained intellectually active and involved. Jobs that offer responsibility and rewards give supernormals a feeling of usefulness, and working part-time, whether volunteer or paid, sustains that feeling, even though these jobs may not be as challenging as their previous careers.[3]

"Youthing" Techniques

As noted, I refer to slowing down, and in some cases the reversing of, the aging process as "youthing." You may have read in other books about various drugs and supplements to control aging; however, I do not recommend that drugs be taken for this purpose.

"Youthing" Imagery

For this exercise, you will need two photographs of yourself. The first should be of you at a much younger age, when you were healthy and vigorous. The second photo is to be a very recent one.

While in hypnosis, using one of the induction techniques already presented, concentrate on the picture of you at a younger age. Visualize your body (a particular part or organ) undergoing a change to recreate this youth in your current body. Do this for at least 10 minutes.

Now, switch to the more recent photograph and repeat this procedure. Imagine an actual positive "youthing" change taking place in your body. Practice this exercise daily, and change your focus to a different part of the body every seven days.

A Self-Hypnosis Exercise

These next exercises require you to do some time traveling. Work on these exercises one at a time, first by placing yourself in self-hypnosis by playing your tape.

The purpose of these exercises is to program positive, longevity-boosting, and health-affirming paths to replace any negative images you may currently hold about your future. By seeing yourself as energetic, active, and healthy, you are slowing down the aging process. If you see a negative image about aging, say to yourself, "That doesn't apply to me, because I am programming my subconscious to initiate my youthing regimen now."

- *Imagine the most significant change you will make in your life after age 75.*
- *Visualize where you will be living and who your friends are when you are 85.*
- *Perceive yourself celebrating your 95th birthday.*
- *See yourself doing your favorite exercise or workout regimen at age 100.*
- *Focus on your greatest accomplishment at age 110.*
- *Describe in detail what your life will be like in the years 2025 and 2045.*
- *Think about which part of your life will be more interesting and more fulfilled in 30 years, 50 years.*
- *Decide what age (at least 120) you will live to reach in a healthy and optimistic manner.*

With this background, practice the following self-hypnosis exercise to slow down and even reverse the aging process.

You are now in a deep hypnotic trance, and from this level you can improve the immune system of your physical body and slow down and even reverse the process of aging. You are in complete control and able to access the limitless power of your subconscious mind. I want you to be open and flow with this experience.

At this time, I would like you to ask your subconscious to facilitate an emotional cleansing and an increase in all levels of the physical body's immune system. You are now slowing down the body's aging process. Do this now.

PLAY NEW AGE MUSIC FOR THREE MINUTES.

Now, I would like you to allow this natural healing energy to spread throughout your entire physical body. Mentally picture yourself as you currently look, and focus on this image. Your body will now decelerate the normal process of aging. Your immune system will improve and resist diseases. Your adrenal glands will produce more and more DHEA hormone to bring about these desired results. Do this now.

PLAY NEW AGE MUSIC FOR FOUR MINUTES.

You have done very well. Now, I want you to further open up the channels of communication by removing any obstacles and allowing yourself to receive information and experiences that will directly improve your ability to slow down and reverse the aging process and help improve your longevity. Allow yourself to receive more advanced and more specific information from your subconscious to raise the quality of your immune system. Mentally picture yourself as you looked 20 or more years ago. Keep this image focused. Your body will now slow down and even reverse the aging process to accomplish this. Do this now.

PLAY NEW AGE MUSIC FOR FOUR MINUTES.

End your trance as usual.

Case History

Polly

Polly was one of my hypnosis patients early in my career, back in 1977. She was 52 years old in 1977, with a history of arthritis, high blood pressure, high cholesterol, depression, and smoking, and she was 50 pounds overweight.

In addition, Polly never exercised and had precancerous lesions diagnosed on her skin and breasts. There was a high probability of the lesions turning cancerous. Genetics was not on Polly's side; her father died of a stroke at age 54 (he had three heart attacks previously); her mother developed skin cancer, and died of breast cancer at age 56.

I worked with Polly on cleansing (see Chapter 10) and youthing. She achieved only a light hypnotic trance level. Deeper levels of hypnosis are not necessary for cleansing to be effective, and this information greatly relieved her.

Polly expressed concern that her 21-year-old daughter would end up like her. Her daughter Carol was somewhat overweight and exhibited depression. I didn't work with Carol, as she was away at school. A few months later Polly moved to the midwest and did not communicate with me again until June of 1996.

Polly apparently followed my career. She read my books and saw my televised interviews on *Oprah, Donahue,* CNN, *Joan Rivers, Regis,* and other shows. Having taken an executive position with a midwest company (which, fortunately, did not have a mandatory age-65 retirement policy), Polly was kept pretty busy.

She was scheduled to go to Los Angeles for a business conference, and a synchronistic event occurred. Just prior to her leaving, she saw my interview on *Leeza* and decided to look me up while out here on the coast.

You can imagine my surprise when she called. I invited her over to the office for a chat and was amazed at what I observed. This now 71-year-young woman was at least 50 pounds thinner than at our last meeting. She no longer smoked, exercised daily, no longer suffered from arthritis, appeared free of depression, and had an acceptable cholesterol count and blood pressure reading. Most important to her, there were no signs of cancer.

Our conversation was one of the most enjoyable I had had in years. The fact that this rather complex history of chronic aging disorders had been reversed, and that a 71-year-young former patient (who looked 20 years younger) presented herself to me after the synchronicity of viewing me on an NBC daytime talk show, only added to the testimony of the power of consciousness expansion.

One final note about this case had to do with Carol. In 1982, Polly purchased my *Slowing Down the Aging Process* self-hypnosis tape for her daughter as a Christmas present. Carol used this cassette diligently, and followed in her mother's footsteps therapeutically.

Carol lost 25 pounds, became active, and now, at age 40 (Polly showed me a recent photo of her, along with one when Carol was 21), had the appearance of a woman in her late 20's. All this was stimulated by her own consciousness—without ever seeing me—just by playing my tape.

Both Carol and Polly have a long and productive life ahead of them. Their relationship markedly improved after Carol's cleansing experiences. It puts a new twist on the old saying "the family that 'youths' together stays together."

Jerome

In 1985, a 58-year-old trial lawyer named Jerome came to see me. He didn't have a particularly high opinion of hypnosis, but my therapy was highly recommended by one of his colleagues (whose wife I had successfully empowered the previous year).

Jerome lived a high-pressure lifestyle. His practice was very demanding and suited his highly skeptical, arrogant, and argumentative personality. He smoked two packs a day, was 35 pounds overweight, had insomnia, and very poor muscular strength.

In short, Jerome was aging rapidly. His history of crash diets, diet pills, nicotine gum, too much television, and high-calorie dinners out taking its toll. As a divorced man, Jerome also longed for female companionship.

It was not easy to work with him. The combination of his argumentativeness and arrogance, coupled with anger at his degenerating body, tested even my patience. Fortunately, the hypnosis techniques were quickly successful and Jerome acknowledged this positive response as the light at the end of the tunnel.

Explaining self-hypnosis techniques to him was no easy chore. It wasn't that Jerome lacked the intellectual capacity to comprehend the paradigm, his skepticism simply played into his natural defense mechanism's resistance to change.

Jerome was a conscientious man, and kept in touch with me for several months following his relatively short therapy. He reported losing about 15 pounds, giving up smoking, and generally having more energy. A business trip to Los Angeles in 1995 prompted another visit with me.

This trial lawyer was 68 when we met again. Jerome called me when he arrived in Los Angeles to thank me for his "new life." I agreed to meet him for coffee one evening, to see how his new life was going. What I saw was an enthusiastic, trim, and vigorous man who looked like he was in his early 50s. He informed me how he had taken up coin collecting and purchased a German Shepherd. (Jerome had never owned a pet before.)

A question concerning his social life revealed that my former patient was living with his 40-year-young girlfriend. His youthing results were nothing short of astounding. He was no longer argumentative (at least when he was not in court), and the only bone of contention was his awarding far too much credit for his growth on me. His youthing resulted from his actions. I merely trained him.

Final Thoughts

Stress is automatically reduced when we relax the mind and body with self-hypnosis. Without stress, no real aging can occur[4]. The most natural and easy experience anyone can have is that of self-hypnosis. It is only because life is so encumbered with stress—during the waking state—that such relaxation techniques as hypnosis are necessary.

The only requirement in youthing is a willingness to incorporate the very successful techniques and paradigms presented in this chapter. Natural, life-extending procedures are no longer mere speculation. They do work. The question that remains is not if you can attain these most desirable goals, but when?

Death has, for the fist time in history, lost its occult mystique. Stripped of its paralyzing mystery, death becomes merely a biological malfunction, rather than a health process to be feared.

Life, not death, remains the mystery. My true purpose is to enhance life and belittle death by this demystification. Perhaps living to an age of 140, 160, or even 200 is not immortality. Who knows what geneticists and other scientists will develop by then to solve the riddle of why DNA's replication mechanism breaks down with time?

We can slow down, and in some cases reverse, many of the physiological and biochemical declines associated with the process of growing older. You will notice I omitted the term aging from the last statement. The research presented has shown that aging is mostly a state of mind.

Try these techniques and heed the advice given. I will look forward to hearing from you 75, 100, or 150 years from now.

CHAPTER 5

BECOME MORE
CREATIVE

Creativity is a right-brain function that originates from the subconscious. The more you communicate directly with your subconscious, the greater the frequency of accessing the true source of your creativity.

Instead of straining your defense mechanism (or rational mind) to attempt to solve creative problems, why not allow your subconscious to take on this role? Many successful creative minds (Edison, Einstein, and others) have done just that.

The capacity for creativity is unlimited, just as no boundaries exist for self-hypnosis. The right brain can be used for problem solving, intuitive judgment, writing, composing, inventing, and other divinely inspired examples.

The creative process is composed of series of steps as follows:

♦ Motivation—A desire to create something original must be present. The reason for this is unimportant. All that matters is the intensity of this desire.

♦ Preparation—The next step is gathering information through research, experience, or experimentation.

♦ Manipulation—Trial-and-error approaches using this data are conducted to synthesize the material into a new paradigm.

- ◆ Incubation—Ideas need time to mature within the subconscious. While the conscious mind is involved with other activities, the subconscious is busy devising a solution. Recall the incubated dreams of the ancient Greeks.
- ◆ Intimation—A sudden feeling occurs that a solution is imminent.
- ◆ Illumination—The answer is finally understood in a flash of insight. Expressions such as "eureka" or "aha" characterize this step.
- ◆ Verification—The proposed solution is tested, examined, and perfected.

Using Dreams to Increase Creativity

We dream for approximately three hours every night, and with proper guidance this presents an ideal therapeutic environment.

A Self-Hypnosis Exercise

The following script is designed to train you to use nightly REM (rapid eye movement) during the dream cycle to improve creativity. If you are making a tape for someone else, substitute *you* for *I*. If you are recording a script for yourself, use *I* instead of *you*. I have purposely applied both methods to these scripts as a guide.

> *I absolutely have the ability to use my dream levels to obtain positive and practical answers to any questions I have and to maximize my creative talents. I will use this time each night to access my natural creative gifts and access the unlimited power of my subconscious mind. My dreams will now be quite detailed and will impart solutions to problems or goals, and increase my creative talents.*

While in hypnosis, just before going to sleep, review a problem that can be solved with information or advice. Be sure you really care about solving it. Now, say to yourself, *I want to have a dream that will contain information to solve a problem, such as _____. I will have such a dream, remember it, and understand it.* Mentally see yourself doing this.

PLAY NEW AGE MUSIC FOR FOUR MINUTES.

Begin to keep a dream diary. Write down all you can remember of your dreams, and as you keep doing this, you are going to discover that you can recall your dreams better and better, in more and more detail, so that your dream diary will consistently become more detailed and more accurate. These recorded dreams are going to contribute to your creative development, your self-understanding.

> *Knowledge is power, and I am now going to train my subconscious mind to release that knowledge to me so my journal and conscious memories will become filled with this knowledge and add to my creative power. Let my subconscious mind begin by giving me a sample of this knowledge now.*

PLAY NEW AGE MUSIC FOR FOUR MINUTES.

End your trance as usual.

This exercise practiced regularly will often result in dramatic improvements in creative endeavors.

A Self-Hypnosis Exercise

Use the following self-hypnosis exercise to facilitate the development of your creative talents. Practice this script just before falling asleep:

> *I am now in a deep hypnotic trance, and from this subconscious mind level, I may request guidance to increase my creativity. I am in complete control and able to access this limitless power of my subconscious mind. I want to be open and flow with this experience.*

> *At this time, I would like to ask my subconscious to assist me in connecting with someone whom I consider a creative role model in my area of special interest. This person may have appeared to me in previous dreams.*

> *Now, ask this individual for guidance on a project that you are currently working on. Focus on the image of this teacher, and select a rendezvous spot (this could be the sanctuary you created*

previously) for a creative brainstorming session. Trust your subconscious and your own ability to allow any thoughts, feelings, or impressions to come into your subconscious mind concerning this goal. You will remember everything you learn from this meeting upon awakening. Now, let your dream world assist you in your creative development.

End this trance as usual.

A Self-Hypnosis Exercise

This last dream exercise allows you to use the sanctuary technique, or to view the scenes suggested by mentally creating a large television monitor.

Imagine a setting you find most conducive for expressing your creativity. It may be contemplating a project in your study, walking through a meadow, viewing a placid mountain scene, or any other environment that will provide a creative stimulus for you. Let yourself become oriented to the peacefulness and beauty of this place.

Now, focus on an example of the type of work you would like to produce. For example, if you are an artist, perceive yourself in a museum portraying the type of art you create. This might be an art exhibition in a gallery. Use this image to obtain any creative ideas that will assist you in your next project.

Shift this scene to one in which you have created some of your specialty area and observe your work being objectively critiqued. Do not be concerned about the quality of these reviews. The purpose of this exercise is to learn how to improve and tap into your natural creative talents. Do not allow ego or other insecurities to contaminate this experience.

Finally, program your subconscious to repeat this technique during your dreams until you obtain your desired goals.

PLAY NEW AGE MUSIC FOR FOUR MINUTES.

End your trance as usual.

Dream Recommendations

Here are some simple recommendations to use your dreams for creative purposes:

* Develop positive dream images that assist you in your endeavors—Doing so will eliminate the nightmarish elements of your dream, and transform negative components into dream helpers.

* Expose your conscious mind to all forms of art, music, literature, and data from several sources—Attend movies and lectures, travel, and engage in conversations and pursuits that stimulate your thoughts, feelings, and soul.

* Become healthfully obsessed with your topic of special interest—Read everything you can on it. See what others have produced or evaluated about this subject. Develop an emotional intensity to create something new in reference to it.

* Prepare yourself for this endeavor by building up your conscious skills in this field—Take courses, study with experts, and use your direct observation and trial and error to become thoroughly familiar with its basics.

* Spend a minimum of two days focusing in your area of interest—Limit your concentration to this discipline and keep this an intense preparation right up until the moment you fall asleep. It is highly recommended to consciously direct your dream content at this time.

* Somehow ask your subconscious to use the dream state to create a product or to find an ingenious solution to a current problem.

* Extract a solution from the unlimited memory bank of the subconscious.

* Sift through the answer and rearrange it in some original form.

* Present this solution in a dream that is easy to understand.

* Visualize and note all the details of the resulting creative dream—Record these dreams in your journal and make them as concrete and applicable as you can (while being as specific as possible). Your stream of consciousness will be active at this time.

♦ Pay particular attention to your recurrent dreams, as well as those that try to edit or correct your interpretation or actions based on previous dream content.

Obstacles to Creativity

The term *pattern thinking* is applied to the tendency of the brain to fail to notice important differences between what's in front of you and what you've perceived in the past. This tendency can function to interfere with the creative process by interpreting the data the brain registers, assigning a meaning to it, and relating it to what you already know, rather than focusing on producing something new.

Another obstacle to creativity is mental routine. The brain uses programmed thought sequences to process information. When it organizes and manipulates memories by using a sequence of mental steps that occur so fast that they cannot be consciously observed, this mechanism is referred to as *mental routines*. As people become older, this helps to explain a decline in creativity. After a certain point in life, they stop acquiring new mental routines, and they learn to get along with the ones they have developed. This tendency can be overcome by developing mindfulness or focused concentration.

The creative process is a continuum. It is something that can be developed, and, once developed, it always results from and is characterized by an increase in brainpower. Often, the world is slow to accept new ideas. The automobile and the copier machine are two excellent examples. Consider the case of the copier machine. Chester Carlson invented it in 1938, but his company did not introduce it until 1948. And it wasn't until 1968 that the copier machine became standard equipment for business offices.

To become creative requires a thought process that uses unorthodox methods to arrive at solutions to problems. This lateral thinking, as described by Cambridge University professor Edward de Bono, differs significantly from traditional vertical thinking, which is depicted as solving problems through a sequential method of going from one logical step to the next.[1]

Although lateral thinking may be classified as a right-brain activity, and vertical thinking as a left-brain activity, a combination of both (and a synchronized approach) is far more ideal, and will result in greater expansion of brainpower and subsequent creativity.

Self-hypnosis can most certainly be used to apply these principles to the creative process. You always want to allow your thoughts about a goal or problem to flow freely before you discuss it with your colleagues, though this goes against the recommendations most of us were taught. I refer to this as *global assessment*.

Global assessment should be conducted before any brainstorming session. Seeing the big picture—or global assessment—can occur spontaneously during a natural daydream (self-hypnotic) state of mind. For example, creative ideas can occur while driving, exercising, getting dressed, shaving, reading leisurely, running errands, just before falling asleep or immediately upon awakening, waking during the middle of the night, and so on.

To take advantage of these creative insights, I suggest you always carry a pen, paper (or 3 × 5 index cards), or a cassette player that can be used to record these thoughts. Global assessment techniques have the following goals as their purpose:

+ To generate many new ideas.
+ To organize these ideas and turn them into a reality.
+ To remove previous mind-sets and open doors to new ideas.
+ To explore all possible combinations of ideas.

The additional steps I recommend to improve creativity and subsequently increase brainpower are:

1. Define the problem—State the goal in clear terms.
2. Visualize an ideal solution to this problem or goal by looking into the future—Your viewpoint during this step should be as if the problem is already resolved.
3. Brainstorming—Record every thought, regardless of how illogical or ridiculous it may appear. Do not edit or censor the data.

4. Cluster ideas into categories (no more than four) and organize them into a plan.
5. Globally assess these clusters, reorganize, edit, and place data
   into a readable framework.
6. Create a first draft or tentative solution.
7. Revise, synthesize, and finalize this solution—Globally assess this concept and polish it.

Throughout this process, both hemispheres of your brain are functioning. The left brain defines the problem, analyzes data, and finalizes
the solution (steps 1, 4, 6, 7). Your right brain is responsible for visualizing, brainstorming, and globally assessing this information (steps 2, 3, 5).
Always remember that creativity requires that a problem everyone else
has already considered be viewed again, and that a solution be devised
that nobody else has thought of. To do this, the proper questions must be
asked.

Most academic training and societal interactions are designed to instruct people to answer questions, rather than to ask the right questions.
Creative problem-solving and improving brainpower require that the correct questions be asked.

**For example, consider the following questions when seeking creative
solutions:**

- What other ideas come to mind?
- What other materials, ingredients, processes, or components
  could I substitute?
- How can I streamline, condense, or minify this?
- What can I do to add extra value, magnify, exaggerate, or
  extend this?
- How can I rearrange, transpose, or exchange components?
- What reverse sequence would improve on this?
- What other ideas can I combine with this to make it better?

**To be creative, you need to apply certain methods to a specific problem.
The following are approaches that have proved effective:**

- Experimentation—It reportedly took Thomas Edison 10,000 failed experiments before he developed the lightbulb. His famous expression that "genius is 1 percent inspiration and 99 percent perspiration" is sometimes quite relevant. You need to be persistent and stay with a problem, but be creative and flexible enough to arrive at a solution.

- Brainstorming—Brainstorming sessions, whether by yourself or with a group, should be free of criticism. An open examination of the problem from all possible angles is required. Follow-up sessions can be used to select, modify, and improve on the resulting ideas.

- Multiple solutions should always be sought—It is important to suspend judgment until other possible answers are accumulated and recorded. You may find a solution to a complex problem from a combination of existing or evolving technologies. In any event, you can always reject these possible answers later.

- Seek advice and counsel from others—You will find that friends, family, and colleagues possess a fresh and different viewpoint from yours. Gather as much raw data as you can. Solutions often arise from outside sources.

- Serendipity—Every so often, you stumble on the solutions to problems or goals you never knew you had. Inventors have devised useful products as a result of experimentation on completely different projects. Metaphysically, this would be described as synchronicity. As you progress in life, take occasional breaks and review previously unsolved problems and unattained goals. Don't be surprised if you find a serendipitous solution.

- Keep records—I cannot overestimate the value of keeping notebooks, journals, or diaries of your ideas. They may arise at the oddest moments. Take clear notes and keep them. These notes serve as a source of ideas and reminders of inspirations you have had. Record what did work, what didn't, questions, things to try, and so on. You can always rearrange these ideas at your leisure. Keep all of your diagrams, flow charts, and other visual aids in the same section as the corresponding written notes to stimulate your synchronized brain.

- Use problem reversal—Sometimes, the solution to a problem arises out of seeing things in reverse, upside down, backward, or inside out. By stating a problem in reverse, you are attempting to define what something is not. This is a technique designed to redirect your perspective by trying to figure out what everyone else is not doing. For example, if your desire is to earn more money, consider ways to lower your income, and use this as a starting point to accomplish your original goal. When you evaluate the opposite and often negative circumstance, you can more easily discover safeguards, and ways to prevent the opposite of your goal from becoming a reality.

- Storyboarding—Drawing is a right-brain activity. It may take the form of schematics, sketches, block diagrams, or doodles. Regardless of how crude they may appear, drawings focus attention on conveying a precise message. Consider the cartoons found in newspapers and magazines. Aren't they easy to understand?

Using your left hand (right brain) for drawing can facilitate your generation of ideas. Following several episodes of drawing, your collection can now be part of storyboarding. In 1928, Walt Disney and his staff created a storyboarding technique they applied to animation.

This method consisted of pinning drawings on the studio walls in related groups so progress could be evaluated and scenes added or discarded efficiently. This method not only assists in the management of many different ideas, it also stimulates the creative process. Placing your ideas on storyboards enables you to see how one idea relates to another and the big picture of the final product. You can use a corkboard to pin index cards, tape them on a wall, or any other device to spread out the components of your project for easy viewing.

Total immersion in a problem is just one of the many advantages of storyboarding. Many people find it useful to begin with a topic index card or sheet of paper and outline general points and categories. Subheading cards are then used to supplement the ideas that fall within the demand of a certain category. This method was reportedly used by Leonardo da Vinci 500 years ago. I use storyboarding to organize my books. This technique has helped me complete 17 books in 30 months.

Additional Hypnosis Exercise to Increase Creativity

(This exercise is on track 4 of the CD in the back of this book.)

Now that you understand the basics of creative thinking, practice this self-hypnosis exercise before engaging in any type of creative idea generation:

You are now going to begin the process of releasing your natural creative energy. You can unleash your creative talents by tapping into your subconscious mind.

You can now draw creative inspiration from the universe. You feel creative and are creative. It is easy and natural for you to generate creative ideas and solutions.

You are open to all the joy and fulfillment life has to offer. You can appreciate, even more, your natural creative expression and beauty.

The wisdom of the universe is within you. Allow your natural creative talents to flow through your awareness and manifest themselves in your present being. Do this now.

PLAY NEW AGE MUSIC FOR FOUR MINUTES.

You are now deeper and deeper in trance as you access your subconscious and tap into your natural abilities for artistic work, for drawing, or painting, or writing, or sculpting, or any kind of creative work. You easily generate creative and marketable ideas. Program your senses to facilitate bringing your ideas to an actual material form. Now, let your subconscious instruct you on your particular creative interest, and mentally perceive yourself applying your creative talent in a highly developed, personally and professionally fulfilling manner.

Focus your creative energies on a current project, or on one that you have put aside for some time. Increase your determination to its maximum level, and now mentally perceive yourself carrying out this creative project successfully while enjoying this entire process. Do this now.

PLAY NEW AGE MUSIC FOR FOUR MINUTES.

Now, for this last exercise, I want you to see yourself receiving formal recognition for your creative talents. If your goal is to develop your creative talents into a full-time professional pursuit, see yourself being established, rewarded, and fulfilled in this endeavor. Do this now.

PLAY NEW AGE MUSIC FOR THREE MINUTES.

End your trance as usual.

A Self-Hypnosis Exercise

Next, practice this more advanced exercise.

In a few moments, I am going to count from one to 20. As I do so, you will feel yourself accessing your subconscious mind level where you will be able to receive information from this hypnotic level, as if you are rising into the air. Number one, rising up. Two, three, four, rising higher. Five, six, seven, letting information flow. Eight, nine, 10, you are halfway there. Eleven, 12, 13, feel yourself rising even higher. Fourteen, 15, 16, almost there. Seventeen, 18, 19, number 20. Now you are there. Take a moment and orient yourself to this relaxed level of hypnosis.

PLAY NEW AGE MUSIC FOR ONE MINUTE.

You are now in a deep hypnotic trance, and from this relaxed level, you are in complete control and able to access this limitless power of your subconscious mind. I want you to be open and flow with this experience.

At this time, I would like you to ask your subconscious to explore the origin of any issue that has impeded your creativity. Trust your own ability to allow any thoughts, feelings, or impressions to come into your subconscious mind concerning this goal. Do this now.

PLAY NEW AGE MUSIC FOR THREE MINUTES.

You are now going to begin the process of releasing your natural creative energy. You can unleash your creative talents by tapping into your subconscious mind.

You can now draw creative inspiration from the universe. You feel creative and are creative. It is easy and natural for you to generate creative ideas and solutions. You are now establishing a synchronization of both hemispheres of your brain, and this will now work in harmony to improve your creativity and brainpower. You are open to all the joy and fulfillment life has to offer. You can appreciate, even more, your natural creative expression and beauty.

The wisdom of the universe is within you. Allow your natural creative talents to flow through your awareness and manifest themselves in your present being. Do this now.

PLAY NEW AGE MUSIC FOR FOUR MINUTES.

You are now deeper and deeper in trance as you access your subconscious and tap into your natural abilities for artistic work, drawing, painting, writing, sculpting, or any kind of creative endeavor. You easily generate creative and marketable ideas. Program your senses to facilitate bringing your ideas to an actual material form.

Now, let your subconscious instruct you on your particular creative interest and mentally perceive yourself applying your creative talent in a highly developed, personally and professionally fulfilling manner. Focus your creative energies on a current project, or one that you have put aside for some time. Increase your determination to its maximum level and now mentally perceive yourself carrying out this creative project successfully (while enjoying this entire process). Do this now.

PLAY NEW AGE MUSIC FOR THREE MINUTES.

Now, for this last exercise, I want you to see yourself receiving formal recognition for your creative talents. If your goal is to develop your creative talents into a full-time professional pursuit, see yourself being established, rewarded, and fulfilled in this endeavor. Do this now.

PLAY NEW AGE MUSIC FOR FOUR MINUTES.

All right. Sleep now and rest. You did very, very well. Listen very carefully. I'm going to count forward now from one to five. When I reach the count of five, you will be back in the present, you will be able to remember everything you experienced and reexperienced. You'll feel very relaxed and refreshed, and you'll be able to do whatever you have planned for the rest of the day or evening. You'll feel very positive about what you've experienced, and very motivated about your confidence and ability to play this tape again to maximize your creativity.

Final Thoughts

Creativity can be greatly increased by expanding use of the right brain through hypnosis. This time-tested and ancient method has always been used in some form to expand human horizons.

CHAPTER 6

IMPROVE YOUR
CONCENTRATION AND MEMORY

In chapter 4, the role of the hormone DHEA in building up the immune system to slow down and even reverse the aging process was discussed. As noted, DHEA is produced from cholesterol and is eventually converted into sex hormones (estrogen for women and testosterone for men). Although it is in its intermediate form as DHEA, it plays a significant role in maintaining the function of brain cells, and may prevent neuronal loss and damage and improve concentration and memory.

Unfortunately, production of this priceless hormone reaches it peak during our 20s, and by the time we are in our 70s, we produce only 10 percent to 20 percent of this peak level. The use of self-hypnosis has been shown to inhibit this decline, accelerate cognitive functions, and slow down and even reverse the normal process of aging.[1]

Studies have demonstrated that patients with Alzheimer's disease and multi-infarct dementia had lower serum levels of DHEA than control groups. The researchers concluded that DHEA may relieve amnesia that contributes to dementia, or is caused by it.[2]

Other research has revealed that even small amounts of DHEA were found to lessen amnesia and enhance long-term memory in mice. From these studies, the scientists concluded that DHEA plays an important role in memory and other cognitive functions. It appears that even very low levels of DHEA can increase the number of neurons in the brain, as well as their ability to establish contact with other neurons and function in higher order mental processes.[3]

The Workings of the Brain

The left brain deals primarily with information that can be represented in sequential or linear form. Such inputs include sequences of sounds, words and sentences, the repetitive features of visual patterns, written language, numbers, and logical if-then relationships. As discussed, the left brain seems to focus on verbal thought, linear sequences, numbers, mathematical relationships, logical chains of reasoning, and time relationships.

On the other hand, the right brain concerns itself with whole forms, especially visual and spatial structures, rather than elements in a sequence. The right hemisphere contains your subject body image—the sense of your physical boundaries, your visual image of your appearance in a mirror, and the relative positioning of your arms, legs, and other body parts at any instant. In addition, the right brain seems to emphasize visual and spatial data much more than the left brain does. Spatial perception and spatial problem-solving are primarily right-brain functions.[4]

The left brain appears more active during most waking activities, whereas the right brain is relatively passive. The reverse is true during waking daydreams and nocturnal dreams (REM cycle). Such functions as singing synchronize both brain hemispheres, with the right brain supplying the subjective sense of rhythm and melody and the left brain supplying the words and operating the larynx.

Information flows freely back and forth between the two hemispheres by means of signals passing across a connecting bridge-like band of nerve factors called the *corpus callosum*. Without a corpus callosum, the two hemispheres would need to operate in isolation.

Any activity that causes the brain hemispheres to function simultaneously results in both a brain synchronization and increased brainpower. Hypnosis is one such activity that facilitates this synchronization.

Although everyone has a complete range of mental abilities, most people think of themselves as innately skilled in only a few of these areas and inherently unskilled in the others.

It has been shown that a synchronization of these two halves of the brain can be manifested at any age. This synchronization of the left and right brain is the key to increased brainpower, and the basis of my hypnosis techniques and the tapes I produce.

The greatest creative minds of this century functioned by this brain synchronization. Examples abound, with Edison, Einstein, and Picasso being three well-known, successful students of this paradigm. In addition, many scientists have come across their breakthrough ideas while daydreaming, and most of the great artists and musicians have been found to be incredibly organized and analytical, especially in relation to their work.[5]

For example, Einstein visualized himself traveling through the universe on a beam of light and, from this perspective, developed the theory of relativity by imagining what took place when matter traveled near the speed of light.[6] Other physicists devised experiments to determine what would happen at the limits of very small sizes and subatomic particles and discovered the laws of quantum mechanics (also known as quantum physics, or the "new physics").

By far, the best example of brain synchronization capabilities was Leonardo da Vinci. In my opinion, this genius was the world's greatest artist, sculptor, physiologist, engineer, anatomist, and inventor. The notebooks for his scientific ideas are very right-brained, containing many three-dimensional images. The final plans of his great artistic masterpieces were almost pure examples of architectural planning: straight lines, angles, numbers, and curves. The left-brain characteristics just mentioned, combined with their complementary right-brain examples, illustrated da Vinci's own ability to utilize both sides of his brain together to maximize his creativity.

Each one of us needs this balance between the left and right brain, and, if it is not achieved, we become relatively ineffective and exhibit poor brain power. It is essential to ensure that the two sides of the brain are actively balanced to benefit from its unlimited potential.

In performing any intellectual or problem-solving work, it is essential to allow the left brain to gather the information and data, and then to allow the right brain the appropriate environment, rest, and solitude to perform its essential part of the process. Finally, both halves of the brain must be synchronized to work in harmony to maximize brainpower. That is the basis of any method of self-hypnosis I employ.

The brain can continue actively for 20 minutes to 60 minutes before it becomes drained of oxygen and requires rest. This thinking organ requires proper management of the rest/activity cycle to continue functioning at full force. Rest is a process in which your brain recuperates, reorganizes, integrates, makes things complete, and prepares for the next left-brain activity cycle.

People describe lack of concentration as one of their main mental difficulties, not realizing that those occasional or regular drifts into daydreams are actually the brain protecting itself against undue wear and tear. You need those little daydreams during the day. Often, when you lose concentration, it is your brain telling you that it is time to take a needed break. These mental breaks are self-hypnotic states and result in increased brainpower.

Within the context of therapy, heightened hypnotic concentration has value as an inherent aspect of trance and is a partial explanation of the effectiveness of hypnotic suggestion. In addition, specific issues (such as improved study habits and various achievement goals ranging from public speaking to improved sports performance) are addressed directly by this hypnotic phenomenon. The subject can actually reenter a state of self-hypnosis later while studying or performing, to gain further value from the concentration inherent to the hypnotic state.

Although sometimes directly associated with concentration (as in some of the previous examples), heightened recall during hypnosis has many functions. Recall of significant events, whether or not they were previously repressed, can be combined with many therapeutic modalities. Also, many persons have used hypnotic access to buried memories to find missing objects of value. Although the use of hypnosis for solving crimes has been restricted in recent years by the courts, hundreds of crimes have been solved by the use of forensic hypnosis, such as when Ed Ray's hypnotic recall of the license plate after the 1976 Chowchilla kidnapping in California led investigators to the kidnappers. Victims and witnesses to crimes have hypnotically recalled crucial memories, whether buried because of detail, time, or trauma.

A person can be taught to reenter hypnosis to access stored memories while taking examinations or, in certain situations, to improve job effectiveness. Therefore, persons developing memory recall skills are supported by the value of increased suggestibility during the initial hypnosis sessions, as well as by the later heightened concentration and recall natural to the state of self-hypnosis. Other values of hypnosis will also apply to improved recall, such as suggestions for text anxiety.

Using a Screen to Increase Brainpower

Using imagery techniques works well to increase our brainpower.

A Self-Hypnosis Exercise

Practice the following script to enhance your brainpower:

> *Imagine a screen in your mind's eye divided into three sections or panels. On the center panel, visualize your mind functioning at its maximum potential. On the left panel, project factors that have compromised your concentration, memory, and other cognitive abilities. The right panel contains your subconscious mind's maximum ability to function as a perfect computer.*
>
> *Now, imagine the right panel completely obliterating the left panel and finally merging with the center panel. Only the center panel illustrating your new increased brain power is now visible. Concentrate on this image and make this your new reality.*
>
> *PLAY NEW AGE MUSIC FOR FOUR MINUTES.*
>
> *End your trance as usual.*

A Time-Distortion Method

It has been reported many times that individuals who have faced certain death-defying situations perceived their lives flashing before their eyes in a matter of seconds just before these events. In addition, dream studies have demonstrated that one minute in dream world can seem like hours in the waking world, and vice versa.

Learning through the use of hypnotically induced time-distortion techniques results in greater efficiency, mostly resulting from the lack of distraction commonly encountered by the conscious mind proper (left brain). High-speed readers (more than 2,000 words per minute) experience this sense of time distortion as data appear to flash through their minds in just a few seconds.

Time-distortion methods can be used to form well-established associative patterns by studying material in this mental state. Because this method offers the opportunity to view problems and goals from all angles instantly, anything can be learned at a rapid rate. This method can be used to memorize speeches, perform high-speed calculations, solve complicated problems, and practice athletic tasks.

A Self-Hypnosis Exercise

Practice this exercise and follow it up by studying something you have put off in the past.

Play a tape of metronome beats striking at a rate of 60 beats per minute. Soon, you will notice your heartbeat slow down to this same rate. Breathe deeply and clear your mind of any extraneous thoughts. Focus on the following statements:

- *The beats of the metronome are slowing down as I become aware of longer and longer time intervals between each beat.*
- *I feel more and more relaxed as strokes become farther and farther apart.*
- *Time is now slowing down...slowing down...slowing down.*
- *I am a good student and enjoy studying.*

- *I remember what I learned.*
- *My mind will give me any information I desire.*
- *Learning is fun and easy.*
- *My intuition allows me to learn faster.*
- *My mind will always present information to me when I need it.*
- *Each time I practice this technique my learning efficiency improves.*
- *I am more confident about increasing my brainpower with each practice session with this tape.*
- *I have plenty of time to use this method to accomplish this learning task. Visualize yourself successfully accomplishing this goal.*

  PLAY NEW AGE MUSIC FOR FOUR MINUTES.

  End your trance as usual.

A Morning Exercise

The following script is designed to speed up the process of tapping into your subconscious and significantly increasing your brainpower. I recommend you practice this upon arising.

Every day you are increasing your ability to learn faster. As your learning ability accelerates, you remember what you learn. You easily assimilate complicated information. You think faster and more precisely. You now learn rapidly. You are an accomplished speed reader. Your eyes vertically sweep a column of type and vertically sweep the page. There is no limit to your reading speed. You retain and recall everything.

Your memory is improving, and you remember everything that is important and desirable for you to retain. You are developing a photographic memory. You focus your concentration at will and always remain alert and attentive when exposed to data of any type. It is easy for you to block out potential distractions that may interfere with your learning.

Your mind and brain have no limits to learning. You can instantly comprehend complicated data and understand it more easily each day. You are always viewing yourself as a winner, and increasing the amount of dendrites in your brain (and other chemical and physiological processes) to tap into your unlimited brainpower. You can do anything that you want to do. Now, I would like you to see yourself applying each of these principles and dramatically increasing your brainpower. Do this now.

PLAY NEW AGE MUSIC FOR FOUR MINUTES.

Now, I would like you to perceive yourself engaging in abstract reasoning and problem-solving, mathematics, science, and anything you desire to study and learn. Imagine your brain actually increasing the number of dendrites each and every day. As you expand your brainpower, you are always synchronizing both sides of your brain in all mental functions. Do this now.

PLAY NEW AGE MUSIC FOR FOUR MINUTES.

End your trance as usual.

By exercising our brain and synchronizing it through self-hypnosis, we can achieve peak experiences and exhibit efficiency and mental powers far beyond our wildest dreams. Focusing the power of your mind on one idea at a time, the essence of self-hypnosis, is a forceful way to increase your brainpower. With practice you can continue the ultimate potential of your conscious and subconscious minds, and make powerful changes in your life.

CHAPTER 7

ELIMINATE
CHRONIC PAIN

Chronic pain is the most common ailment that brings people into medical offices and hospitals today. Modern medicine simply cannot cure this symptom, and merely prescribes medications that are addictive and have several other negative side effects. Interestingly, many physicians are now recommending hypnosis for the permanent relief of various types of chronic pain.

Hypnosis is effective in eliminating any kind of pain, from tension headaches to pain from muscles, joints, and even from terminal cancer.

The following types of chronic pain can be alleviated by using self-hypnosis:

- Muscle pain.
- Neck pain.
- Facial pain.
- Sexual pain.
- Post-operative pain.
- Stomach pain.
- Herpes zoster (shingles).
- Tension headaches.
- Migraine headaches.
- Phantom-limb pain.

- Tendinitis.
- Arthritis.
- Back pain.
- Cancer.
- Neuralgia.
- Colitis.
- Sciatica.
- Ulcers.
- Jogging pain.
- Fibromyalgia.
- Chronic-fatigue syndrome.

Anyone can be trained to use self-hypnosis to relieve the symptoms and causes of chronic pain. When applying this time-tested method for chronic pain elimination, even though intellectually you are aware that pain is present, you do not register the discomfort. It is possible to create imaginary numbness or tingling sensations with the mind to filter out the hurt from the body's pain. Other advantages of using self-hypnosis include developing a better self-image, losing weight, developing better muscle tone, increasing endurance, slowing down the aging process, improving levels of activity, decreasing anxiety, tension, depression, or anger, and, most important, creating a new lifestyle free of pain.

Pain experienced for less than three months is referred to as *acute pain*, whereas discomfort lasting more than three months is termed *chronic pain*. Acute pain is actually a useful diagnostic tool in that it pinpoints a problem, has a rapid onset, lasts a short time, and resolves itself either naturally or with some form of treatment. Chronic pain, on the other hand, fails to respond to treatment, results in a merry-go-round of medical referrals, possible addiction to medication, and severely compromises the patient physically, mentally, emotionally, and spiritually.

With chronic pain, the discomfort occupies center stage of a patient's life. It causes an individual's social life, work, sports, personal relationships, and other activities to revolve around the pain. Both endurance and activity decline. The self-image is lowered and anxiety levels soar.

Anxiety produces more pain, which produces more anxiety, which produces more pain—and a vicious cycle is established. Chronic pain has become a serious national problem, and is the most common cause of disability in the United States today.

The amount of pain felt in any circumstance varies with the intensity of the experience, but it is not necessarily proportional. Professional athletes have demonstrated that even bones broken during the tension of a game may be experienced as entirely painless, whereas stepping on a tack can be accompanied by intense pain. The individual's state of mind, physical health, and tolerance to pain also play a part in the experience of pain. In addition, alcohol or other drug consumption, anger, sexual excitement, or a state of shock affect the actual manifestation of pain.

Specific characteristics of an individual's makeup can increase susceptibility to pain. Do the following characteristics of pain susceptibility fit you?

- Increased feelings of guilt.
- Reduced sexual interest or activity.
- Increased anxiety.
- Increased irritability.
- Thoughts of suicide.
- Insomnia.
- Inability to concentrate, or poor concentration.
- Decreased tolerance for pain.
- Increased fatigue.

These characteristics often lead to what I term the *vicious cycle of pain*. Consider the following paradigm.

Pain...anger...depression...medication...more pain...frustration...an increase of medication...addiction...increased frustration...increased depression...more doctors...possible surgery...lower tolerance to pain...increased medication...increased depression...increased frustration...more pain...and the cycle repeats itself.

Through self-hypnosis, you can learn to relax and be more comfortable in any situation. You can use imagery to help you tap inner strengths and find hope, courage, patience, perseverance, love, and other qualities that can help you eliminate the cause of chronic pain.

Conditions, such as anxiety, that are caused or aggravated by stress often respond well to imagery techniques. The emotional aspects of any discomfort can often be alleviated through imagery, and relieving the emotional distress may in turn encourage you to become more empowered and permanently resolve your chronic pain.

A Self-Hypnosis Exercise

Practice the following pain and healing exercise to begin your elimination of discomfort.

As you relax more and more in self-hypnosis, the relaxation causes all the muscles and nerves in the affected area to become completely relaxed, thereby relieving the symptom and causing the pain to disappear. As you become more and more relaxed in every way, you return to normal functioning, and your body feels completely comfortable and free from all discomfort.

You are becoming desensitized in the various parts of your body where you have been complaining of pain. You will now find yourself recovering rapidly, with the healing process being greatly facilitated as a result of your recruitment of nature's healing forces. Naturally, the pain will not stop all at once. Deepen your trance by taking a deep breath and saying to yourself "20, 20, 20." The act of counting is a post-hypnotic suggestion intended to relieve the discomfort. The act of counting will cause you to become desensitized and anesthetized in those parts of the body where you are uncomfortable, and you will rapidly resume a relaxed and comfortable condition. You will also find yourself pleasantly hungry, and at mealtimes will be able to eat well and hold your food down satisfactorily. (This latter suggestion is given if the individual is experiencing nausea.) You are steadily losing your susceptibility for pain and discomfort.

Feel yourself becoming a loving and forgiving person. Consider love as an end in itself. Express your desire to achieve a thorough mental house cleaning...use positive words and thoughts to become a loving, forgiving person.

Imagine the illness or pain bothering you. Focus your healing energies. Quickly erase this image of your illness and see yourself as being completely cured. Feel the freedom and happiness of being in perfect health. Hold on to this image, linger over it, enjoy it, and know that you deserve it. Know that now, in this healthy state, you are fully in tune with nature's intentions for you.

Every day, in every way, you are getting better, better, and better. Negative thoughts and suggestions have no influence over you at any mind level.

A Visual-Imagery Exercise

Now, move on to this visual-imagery script model that was presented in Chapter 2:

You are a free and powerful being who, beginning today, will eliminate once and for all any chronic pain. Your body and mind will heal and balance itself. You have all of the inner strength necessary to create your new reality free of chronic pain.

You are in control of your life and are confident about your ability to permanently eliminate chronic pain from your reality. Every day, you are programming your subconscious to accomplish this goal. You unconditionally love and accept yourself and desire to free yourself of chronic pain once and for all. You have the self-discipline to accomplish your personal and professional goals. Every day, in every way, you increase your self-discipline. You do what you need to do and stop doing what doesn't work. You now adapt and you keep pace with the movements of change. You always consider your options, and you always act in your own best interest. You are self-reliant and self-confident. You are filled with independence and determination. You project a very positive self-image. You can do whatever you set your mind to.

Mentally see an image of yourself standing before you. This is your body exactly as you would like it to appear, free of any and all chronic pain. Examine it more and more closely now, and it will be a realistic, but ideal, body image, one that you really could achieve, and one that you will achieve. And when you have a very clear image of your body as you would like to have it, keep observing that image, and make it a part of your own reality.

PLAY NEW AGE MUSIC FOR TWO MINUTES.

That ideal body image is becoming more and more real. You are seeing it very clearly, and seeing it in its full size and dimensions. And now that you are going to step forward and into that body, you will find yourself in that body, so that you can try it out and make certain that it is just the body you do want to have. And if there is something you would like to change, make those changes now. See yourself free from all chronic pain.

Move around in that body, feel its strength and agility, its dynamic aliveness, its surging vitality, and make really certain that its appearance and all its attributes are what you realistically desire. And as you occupy that body, coming to know that body very well, your present physical body is going to be drawn into that new mold. You are already moving toward the realization of that ideal body image, and you will be doing whatever is needed to achieve the body you want to have. You are completely free of all chronic pain.

PLAY NEW AGE MUSIC FOR FOUR MINUTES.

End your trance as usual.

Glove Anesthesia

If your pain is limited to a small area of the body, an approach that works well is called *glove anesthesia*. This method consists of mentally numbing one hand and transferring that feeling of numbness to the painful area.

A Self-Hypnosis Exercise

Practice the following script to master this pain-control technique:

All feeling is going to disappear from your right hand. You will not be able to feel anything in your right hand. Just think of your right hand becoming quite numb, as if it had gone to sleep. Gradually, it is becoming more and more numb and all the feeling is going out of it.

And as I go on talking to you, your right hand is beginning to feel colder and colder, as if it were surrounded by ice. Just picture your right hand being packed in ice, and as you do so, it is feeling colder and colder, more and more numb and insensitive. Your right hand has now become so cold and numb that you are losing all feeling in it. Soon, you will not be able to feel any sensation in it at all.

In a moment or two I am going to count slowly to three. And when I reach the count of three, your right hand will be completely insensitive to pain and you will be able to feel no pain at all in your hand. One, losing all sensation of pain. Two, your hand is now quite numb and dead, there is no feeling in it at all, just as if it had gone to sleep. Three, your hand is completely numb, cold, and insensitive. You cannot feel any pain in it at all.

Now, use your right hand to touch any part of your body that is painful. By doing so, all this cold, numb feeling from your right hand and fingers will be transferred to this part of your body. Do it now.

*In a few moments, your right hand will become quite normal
again. It is becoming warmer and warmer, and the feeling of numbness is leaving it, and it is quite normal again, just the same as
your other hand.*

Research from pain clinics has revealed that glove anesthesia techniques have been quite effective, even when pain medication has failed.

Pain Symbols

Studies have shown that the brain assigns certain shapes and colors to
symbolize pain. Visual imagery can be used to create shapes and colors
that counteract this effect. This results in a significant diminishing of
pain.

An image must be created using symbols or colors to represent pain
and pain relief, because feelings cannot be visualized. In effect, pain can
be eliminated by creating a shape and color that are naturally incompatible with those of pain. Here are four easy techniques for obtaining your
pain object and pain color.

The Disappearing Blimp

Use the following script to determine your pain symbol and color:

*Using a deep breathing technique, relax yourself and visualize
a large TV screen like you might see in a stadium. This screen is
showing a view of the infield, but you can't see it because a
Goodyear blimp is blocking your view. On the infield lies your
pain symbol and color (represented by a colored cloth on the
grass). The blimp now moves away and your pain symbol and
color are revealed.*

Seeing Behind the Screen

*Relax yourself and imagine yourself in a theater. The curtain
is closed, and you are told that your pain symbol and color are
on the stage behind it. Slowly open the curtain in your mind's eye
and note your personal pain symbol and color.*

Practice the following exercise to apply this method:

Visualize the shape and color of your pain. It may resemble any geometric shape. Whatever shape comes to your mind is the answer. Now perceive the color of this shape. This is your pain color.

Now, make your pain symbol this color and project it out 10 feet in front of you. Systematically alter the shape of your pain symbol to other geometric forms and meditate on each form for five seconds. Repeat this method with your pain color.

Recreate your original pain symbol and color and enlarge it to 10 times its original size. Now, change its shape quickly to at least five other forms. Repeat this method by changing its color to at least five other hues.

Next, shrink your pain symbol to twice its original size and repeat this procedure. Finally, bring your pain symbol down to its original size and repeat this procedure. End this exercise by dissolving your pain symbol and color and opening your eyes.

Creating a Pain-Relief Object and Color

To determine your pain-relief symbol and color, use either the disappearing blimp or seeing-behind-the-curtain method. Another way to make this determination is to simply identify what is most incompatible with your pain symbol and color. For example, a circle is incompatible with a cube and red contrasts with green.

Creating a Sanctuary

Any relaxing scenery can be most effective in eliminating chronic pain. This can be a real place or one that has been created. I call this your *sanctuary*. The simple act of visualizing your sanctuary can eliminate most types of chronic pain. Breathe slowly and deeply as you practice this technique.

Sit back, relax, breathe deeply, and send a warm feeling into your toes and feet. Let this feeling break up any strain or tension, and as you exhale let the tension drain away. Breathe deeply and send this warm feeling into your ankles. It will break up any strain or tension, and as you exhale let the tension drain away. Breathe deeply and send this feeing into your knees, let it break up any strain or tension there, and as you exhale let the tension drain away. Send this warm sensation into your thighs so any strain or tension is drawn away. Breathe deeply and send this warm feeling into your genitals and drain away any tension.

Send this warm feeling into your abdomen now; all your internal organs are soothed and relaxed and any strain or tension is draining away. Let this energy flow into your chest and breasts; let it soothe you, and as you exhale any tension is draining away. Send this energy into your back now. This feeling is breaking up any strain or tension, and as you exhale the tension is draining away. The deep, relaxing energy is flowing through your back, into each vertebra, as each vertebra assumes its proper alignment. The healing energy is flowing into all your muscles and tendons, and you are relaxed, very fully relaxed. Send this energy into your shoulders and neck; this energy is breaking up any strain or tension, and as you exhale the tension is draining away. Your shoulders and neck are fully relaxed. And the deep, relaxing energy is flowing into your arms—your upper arms, your elbows, your forearms, your wrists, your hands, your fingers are fully relaxed.

Let this relaxing energy wash up over your throat, so that your lips, your jaw, your cheeks are fully relaxed. Send this energy into your face so that the muscles around your eyes, your forehead, and your scalp are relaxed. Any strain or tension is draining away. You are relaxed, most completely relaxed.

And now float to your space, leave your physical body, and move between dimensions and travel to your space—a meadow, a mountain, a forest, the seashore—wherever your mind is safe and free. Go to that space now. And you are in your space, the space you have created, a space sacred and apart. Here in this space, you are free from all tension and in touch with the calm, expansive power within you. Here in this space, you have access to spiritual information and energy. Your flow is in harmony with the flow of the universe. Because you are part of the whole creation, you have access to the power of the whole of creation. Here you are pure and free. This is your personal sanctuary.

Now ask yourself, "What are my pain-relief symbol and color?" Stay here for a few minutes and, when you are ready, let yourself drift up and back to your usual waking reality. You will return relaxed, refreshed, and filled with energy. And you will return now, gently and easily. You now have discovered your pain-relief symbol and color and will remember them upon opening your eyes.

This sanctuary method has been utilized successfully by thousands of my patients to relieve pain and grow spiritually.

The Switch-Off Imagery

By first determining what the pain symbol is (a word, hot coal, knife, and so forth) as well as its color, the appropriate pain-relief symbol and color can then be used to neutralize discomfort.

To maximize results, the most effective method is to first determine what the pain looks and feels like, and how to relieve it visually. For example, suppose it has been ascertained that the pain symbol is a corkscrew and its color is red.

It is determined that the most effective way to eliminate this pain is to reverse the direction of the corkscrew and apply a blue (the pain-relief color) salve to the wound in your back.

A Visual-Imagery Exercise

Try this visual-imagery script to eliminate pain with your previously determined symbols.

Feel the pain as the corkscrew is boring into your back in a clockwise direction. See red blood spurting out all around it as you grimace in severe pain. Now, imagine a hand turning the corkscrew in a counterclockwise direction and feel the corkscrew being withdrawn from your back. Say to yourself, "The corkscrew is being withdrawn and the discomfort is lessening."

Next, visualize blue salve being applied to the wound left by the discarded corkscrew. This soothing blue color completely replaces the red color seen earlier. Say to yourself, "The blue salve is numbing my back and the pain is disappearing. I am now free of any discomfort."

All sensation has returned, and you can feel everything in your back as before. The discomfort has been removed by your body's healing processes.

Blackboard Technique

A visual-imagery technique that works well for most people, and utilizes one's imagination, is the blackboard technique.

A Self-Hypnosis Exercise

The following script can be used to apply the blackboard method.

I want you to imagine that you can see a blackboard, and that you are standing in front of it with a piece of chalk in your hand. Just picture that blackboard. Now, as you watch that blackboard, you can see yourself writing on it with the chalk.

You can see what you are writing. You are writing the words "pain free." You can see those words quite clearly. Now, feel the increased relaxation and enjoy this freedom from pain.

PLAY NEW AGE MUSIC FOR THREE MINUTES.

As you continue looking at the blackboard, you now see yourself erasing the words "pain free." And as the words "pain free" disappear from the blackboard, so will your pain also disappear from your mind—just as if your mind were being cleaned like a blackboard. As soon as you can see that the words have disappeared and the blackboard is clear and blank, your state of mind will resume its normal level of conscious awareness.

Age Regression

Many chronic-pain symptoms originate from the repressed emotions of past episodes in life. The use of age regression through hypnosis can bring these feelings to the surface and eliminate these causes from our current awareness, resulting in the reduction or elimination of discomforts.

Try this age regression exercise. It is best practiced as a recorded tape.

Now listen very carefully. In a few minutes, I'm going to be counting backward from 20 to one. As I count backward from 20 to one, you are going to perceive yourself moving through a very deep and dark tunnel. The tunnel will get lighter and lighter, and at the very end of this tunnel will be a door with a bright, white light above it.

When you walk through this door you will appear to be at an earlier age. You're going to reexperience this earlier age and move to an event that will be significant in explaining your present discomfort or the origin of any problem or negative tendency that created this pain.

But before I do that, I want you to realize that if you feel uncomfortable either physically, mentally, or emotionally at any time, you can awaken yourself from this hypnotic trance by simply counting forward from one to five. You will always associate my voice with a friendly voice in trance. You will be able to let your mind review its memory banks and always associate my voice with a friendly voice in trance. You will be able to let your mind review its memory banks and follow the instructions for perceiving the scenes from this earlier age, following along as I instruct.

You'll find yourself able to get into hypnotic trances more deeply and more quickly each time you practice with this tape, or with other methods of self-hypnosis. When you hear me say the words, "Sleep now and rest," I want you to detach yourself immediately from any scene you are experiencing. You will be able to await further instructions.

You absolutely have the power and ability to go back in time, as your subconscious mind's memory bank remembers everything you've ever experienced. I want you to relive these past events only as a neutral observer, without feeling or emotion, just as if you were watching a television show. I want you to choose positive or neutral past experiences. You will be able to remove any obstacles that are preventing you from achieving your most useful, positive, beneficial, and constructive goals.

Go back and explore at least two or three memories of yourself. It doesn't matter how far back you go. It doesn't matter what the years are. I just want you to get used to going backward in time.

I'm going to count backward now from 20 to one. As I do so, I want you to feel yourself moving into the past. You'll find yourself moving through a pitch-black tunnel that will get lighter and lighter as I count backward. When I reach the count of one, you will have opened up a door with a bright white light above it and walked into a past scene. You will once again become yourself at an earlier age.

Now listen carefully. Twenty, you're moving into a very deep, dark tunnel surrounded by grass and trees and flowers, and a very, very inviting atmosphere. You feel very calm and comfortable about moving into the tunnel.

Nineteen, 18, you're moving backwards in time, back, back. Seventeen, 16, 15, the tunnel is becoming lighter now. You can make out your arms and legs, and you realize you are walking through this tunnel and you're moving backward in time.

Fourteen, 13, 12, moving so far back, back. Eleven, 10, nine, you're so far back now, you're more than halfway there. The tunnel is much lighter. You can perceive a brilliant white light around you, and you can now make out a door in front of you with a bright, white light above it.

Eight, seven, six, standing in front of the door now, feeling comfortable and positive and confident about your ability to move into this past scene. Five, four, now walk up to the door and put your hand on the doorknob. The bright white light is so bright it's hard to look at directly.

Three, open the door. Two, step through the door. One, move into the past scene. You are there.

Focus carefully on what you see before you. Take a few minutes now and let everything become crystal clear. The information flowing into your awareness, the scene becoming visual and visible. Just take the time to orient yourself to your environment. Focus on it. Take a few moments and then listen to my instructions. Let the impression form.

PLAY NEW AGE MUSIC FOR 30 SECONDS.

First, what do you perceive and what are you doing? Focus carefully on my voice now. I want you to let any information flowing into your awareness—the scene as well as the actual environment you are in—become clear now. Crystal clear. I want you to focus on yourself. First of all, where you are. Focus on how old you are, how you are dressed, what you are doing there, your purpose there at this particular time, anyone else who is around you (parents, relatives, or friends). I'm going to give you a few moments. I want you to let the scene develop and become clear. Develop and become crystal clear.

PLAY NEW AGE MUSIC FOR FOUR MINUTES.

Sleep now and rest. Detach yourself from this scene now. I want you now to focus on my voice again. I'm going to be counting forward again, this time from one to five. When I reach the count of five, I want you to progress in time by three years. I want you to move at least three years forward in time.

Move to a specific event that is going to happen to you—something that is going to affect you and your development. I want you to move forward to a very significant scene—especially if it involves other people.

On the count of five now, I want you to perceive yourself in this scene just as you did before. One, moving forward, carefully, comfortably, slowly. Two, moving further forward. Three, half-way there. Four, almost there. Five, you are there.

Now focus again. Let the scene crystallize and become clear. Focus on yourself. Where you are? Who you are with? What is happening around you? What has happened since I last spoke with you? Understand the physical setting of the scene. Let it develop. Allow it to relate to your particular problem, or just experience going back in time. Carefully, comfortably allow the scene to unfold. Carefully and comfortably. Now perceive the scene unfolding. Let it unfold now.

PLAY NEW AGE MUSIC FOR FOUR MINUTES.

Sleep now and rest. Listen to my voice. Detach yourself from this scene. You're going to be moving forward one more time.

On the count of five, you're going to be moving forward to a minimum of five years from this time. You will be moving forward to what ideally will be resolution of this problem (or to another significant scene that will affect the development of this problem) or just to an experience of going back in time again.

Moving forward to a minimum of five years from this time on the count of five. Carefully, comfortably. One, moving forward. Two, moving further forward. Three, halfway there. Four, almost there. Five.

Now, again, let the scene crystallize, let it become crystal clear. Focus on what is happening around you. Where are you? Who are you with? What has happened since I last spoke with you? If this is a problem you are resolving, find out exactly what happened, exactly how it was resolved. Find out what additional facts are related to the present problem. Carefully and comfortably let the images flow and the scene become clear. Let go of any discomfort that may have resulted from this event. Do this now.

PLAY NEW AGE MUSIC FOR FOUR MINUTES.

All right, very good. You've done very well now. Sleep and rest. Listen carefully as I count forward again from one to five. On the count of five, you will be back in the present. You will still be in a deep, hypnotic trance, but you will be able to relax comfortably and be free of these scenes. But you will still be in a trance.

One, you're heading forward in time back to the present. Two, further forward. Three, halfway there. Four, almost there. Five.

Listen as I count forward one more time, from one to five. On the count of five, you will be wide-awake, refreshed, relaxed. You will be able to do what you have planned for the rest of the day or evening. You will be able to remember everything you experienced and reexperienced, and be perfectly relaxed and at ease. You will also be able to recreate further experiences of scenes from the past by playing this tape again and again.

One, very, very deep. Two, you're getting a little lighter. Three, you're getting much, much lighter. Four, very, very light. Five, awaken.

Pain can have psychological as well as physical causes. Always seek medical assistance for any discomfort before applying self-hypnosis approaches. Once you have determined that conventional medical treatment has done all it, use the scripts presented in this chapter to reduce, or even eliminate, your discomfort.

CHAPTER 8

MAXIMIZE YOUR
SEX LIFE

To obtain the most out of your sex life, you must attain what I refer to as *sexual bliss*. When you love spiritually and are considerate of your partner in sexual expression, maintain complete honesty, and initiate an intimate connection through sex with another person, you are engaged in the act of sexual bliss.

Having sex is done to someone, not with them. You are using this individual rather than helping or being one with him or her. This physiological and psychological high is neither a meaningful connection nor spiritually based.

Even having sex solely to please another person results in creating users out of sexual partners, whereas you become a usee. It is only when you have sex with someone that you are sexually connecting, intimately and meaningfully, for the purpose of mutual growth and wellness. Only then do you exhibit sexual bliss.

Sexual bliss is far more than genitals and mechanical procedures of seduction, foreplay, sexual aerobics, multiple orgasms, and subsequent release of built-up neuromuscular tension and stress. It is connecting sensually with your own body and that of your lover. This true form of making love involves a physical, mental, emotional, and spiritual connection with your lover that results in a mutual soul healing.

Another characteristic of sexual bliss is being aware of the present moment and its every sensation. This mindfulness is sex in, and not for, the moment. To competently engage in sexual bliss, you must have a type of sexual intimacy that is unrushed. By allowing enough time for this spiritual merging, you can eliminate feelings of guilt, obligation, resentment, distraction, self-recrimination from the past, and other baggage. Hypnosis can be used to achieve these goals.

Preparing for Sexual Bliss

Before I present hypnotic techniques to attain sexual bliss, some final planning is necessary. In the beginning, it is especially important to create an ideal atmosphere for practicing the exercises and techniques presented.

The following is a list of some of these considerations.

1. Arrange in advance to prepare your bedroom for these exercises by selecting sexy night clothes, providing relaxing and sensual music, clean sheets, flowers, candles, light snacks, and lubricant. Add to this list anything else either of you can think of to create a romantic ambiance with spiritual overtones.

2. Learn to express appreciation to your partner. This can be easily accomplished by listing all of his or her positive and attractive traits, and why you feel in love with him or her.

3. Make sure you will not be interrupted during your time together. Arrange for children and animals to be cared for, inform relatives and friends that you cannot be disturbed, turn on the telephone answering machine (turned down so you can't hear the caller), and leave the television and radio off.

4. Discuss only here-and-now topics that are positive and promote mutual enjoyment.

5. Make a pact to respect each other's right to say no to any technique or practice. Adopt the attitude that no mistakes are possible. Delayed orgasms, lost erections, unintended orgasms, and similar encounters are acceptable and will not interfere with sexual bliss aspirations.

6. Prepare a surprise for your partner. This may take the form of a gift or a special sex-enhancing technique.

7. Allot some time for reflection and privacy. Respect each other's right to be silent and introspective.

8. Adopt a policy of honesty and healthy communicative skills.

It is important to practice these simple recommendations before moving on to the more advanced methods depicted later on.

Patience is always a prerequisite for attaining any worthwhile goal. Sexual bliss is no exception.

Preparing Your Mind for Sexual Bliss

These exercises are designed to facilitate communication with your partner, create and develop a spiritual bond, and remove any inhibitions toward experiencing pleasurable sexual sensations and learning more about each other's sexual desires.

A Self-Hypnosis Exercise

For this first exercise, sit in a different room than your partner. You both can be fully clothed, completely nude, or anything in between.

Close your eyes and try to communicate with your partner telepathically. Relax your muscles and focus on your breathing. Try to sense and feel your partner's presence in the other room.

Now, send out seductive thoughts to your partner. Concentrate on certain signals that indicate sexual arousal when you are in each other's presence. Send out strong mental sex messages that you are desirous of passionate sex. Be specific in your imagery.

End the session in 20 minutes. Now have your partner communicate telepathically with you. Do not discuss your thoughts until after he or she completes these steps.

Recalling the Most Fulfilling Sexual/Spiritual Liaison

An exercise that fastens a spiritual bond between partners is carried out by each recalling his or her most fulfilling sexual encounter.

A Self-Hypnosis Exercise

This exercise can be conducted alone or with your partner. I suggest playing New Age or other types of soft, soothing background music during this exercise.

Relax, close your eyes, and breathe deeply. Mentally create an impression of the most stimulating and fulfilling sexual encounter you had with your partner. This may include or be replaced by a spiritual encounter that resulted in a special bonding between the two of you.

Bring forth any visual images, thoughts, feelings, or other sensations that were a part of this experience. If it was a time you both were intimate, recall as many of the details as possible. Let these images stay with you for at least seven minutes.

Now, place your consciousness in this imagery and act as if it were happening now. Your mind may create any reality it desires. If you believe this liaison is occurring now, it is!

During this visualization and reexperiencing of this blissful time, allow any associated pleasurable sensations to express themselves. Observe every detail, from the room or landscape to the shape of your lover's body. Recall the conversation, the weather, your partner's scent; become immersed in this sensory reenactment.

Open your eyes when you are finished. If your partner is present, let him or her try this exercise. Share your experience with your lover and end this method with a long hug and mutual expression of appreciation for each other.

Breathing Exercises to Attain Sexual Bliss

Proper breathing assists greatly in focusing your concentration and in oxygenating your body so both the stamina and quality of the sexual union will be enhanced. Unfortunately, most of us breathe too quickly and too shallow.

A Self-Hypnosis Exercise

Deep breathing is the key to these exercises. Practice these exercises regularly to acquire the technique of proper breathing.

Stand upright, keeping your arms relaxed at your sides and your feet apart. Breathe normally through your nose with your mouth closed. Place both hands, one over the other, on your abdomen just below your navel. Breathe in deeply and distend your stomach muscles by taking in air, not by muscular force.

Breathe out and press both hands gently against your abdomen until all of the air has been released. Repeat this five times to constitute one cycle. Breathe normally for four breaths, and repeat the entire cycle four additional times.

Repeat this procedure, except now breathe mainly from the chest.

When you practice these exercises enough times regularly, your body will become so conditioned that with one smooth inhalation, the air is directed into your fully expanded chest, leaving some room in your abdomen. As you continue breathing in, the abdomen fills up with air.

The reverse occurs on breathing out. Most of the air in the chest is now released and, subsequently, the air from the abdomen. Next, the remaining air in your chest, and finally your abdomen, is let go. To summarize, breathing in—aspiration—can be described as: abdomen-chest-abdomen-chest. Expiration—breathing out—is characterized by: chest-abdomen-chest-abdomen.

Men typically have more difficulty with breathing from the chest. They favor abdominal breathing. Women, on the other hand, find abdominal breathing more challenging because they tend to breathe from the chest.

To obtain the maximum benefits from this approach, continual practice is required. Practice will quickly illustrate that this deep breathing technique is the natural way to breathe.

You can expect the following benefits from deep breathing:

- Increased concentration.
- Relaxation.
- Heightened vitality.
- Calmness.
- Increased confidence.
- Increased stamina.

Improper breathing limits the sensations one may experience during sex. It may even prevent an orgasm.

The Consciousness of Sexual Bliss

It must be understood that the conscious mind, unless specific trans-formation techniques are being applied, is stabilized. This means that it maintains its integrity, despite the continual alterations in the body and surrounding world. For example, individual identity is still acknowledged, even if a sudden noise or other distraction is perceived.

Evolution has something to do with this system. If a state of cosmic consciousness were entered whenever a certain stimulus presented itself, survival in both primitive and current times would be difficult. Sunlight bouncing off the hood of a car while you are crossing the street could result in instant death if you failed to get out of the path of the car.

Much of the stabilization of ordinary consciousness comes about through the load—that is, the work that all these processes impose on awareness. Because doing this work is almost completely automated, it ordinarily does not feel like hard work to maintain such an ordinary state; it just seems to be.

Another component of consciousness is referred to as *statespecificity*.[1] This implies that certain aspects of knowledge can't be known unless you are in a certain particular state of consciousness. When you enter into an orgasmic level of awareness, an altered state of consciousness is created.

By raising consciousness, the state of being can be altered and individu-als can be transformed into stronger, more intelligent, sensitive, loving, and more orgasmic beings. Another advantage of this spiritual evolution is to enhance the depth of intimacy and love in all existing relationships. With these same characteristics, new relationships will develop as well.

As you become absorbed in ecstatic sensations, past and future seem to disappear. This functioning in the now alters the usual thought patterns and tendency toward critical and analytical thinking. Physiologically, the body becomes energized and inundated with pleasurable sensations of sexual bliss. Biochemically, serotonin and endorphins are produced, resulting in a state of well-being and a natural high.

A state of sexual bliss is approached as all boundaries between you and your lover disappear. Now, a oneness with the universe joins this harmony with your partner. Other cultures have attempted to create this state by means of chanting, drumming, special breathing techniques, danc-ing, and ingesting aphrodisiacs. This common goal is to awaken orgasmic, sexual energy. Easterners would describe this mechanism as the raising of the kundalini. My main thesis is that everyone is capable of transforming sexual energy, and directing and expanding it to create a state of sexual bliss.

Here are some recommendations that will assist you in guiding your consciousness toward sexual bliss.

- Be at one with the infinite scheme of things. Practice self-hypnosis and meditation to attain this goal.
- Eliminate negative foods, drink, drugs, and toxic emotions from your life.
- Pay attention to your intuition and spiritual insights.
- Remember that everyone you meet, whether it is a positive or negative experience, is merely a projection of your consciousness. It is what you most dislike that you most deny in yourself. What you most desire is what you most wish for in yourself. Use this to guide your spiritual growth.
- Eliminate the tendency to judge yourself and others.
- Do not seek external approval.
- Live life in the current moment and appreciate it fully. Let go of the past and do not worry about the future.
- Let go of all anger. Doing so will facilitate your own healing and retard the aging process.
- Be motivated by love, rather than by fear.
- Be empowered.

Never separate the concept of consciousness from your sexuality. Without consciousness, sexual bliss is impossible.

Removing Obstacles to Sexual Bliss

Our diet and prescription drugs we take can function as an impediment to attaining sexual bliss.

The following are recommendations for removing obstacles to sexual bliss.

- Cut down on your alcohol intake. The greater the intake of alcohol, the more problematic sex becomes. Alcohol lowers the testosterone level in men, creating potency problems; in women it delays orgasms.

- Add more zinc to your diet. Zinc is helpful in maintaining male sexual health and vigor. Smoking and drinking deplete the ability to absorb zinc. Liver, sunflower seeds, oats, nuts, and cheese are good sources of zinc.

- Exercise regularly. The more active you are, the greater your vigor and interest in sex—both mentally and physically.

- Cut down on sweets. Hypoglycemia (low blood sugar) has been correlated with potency problems in men and orgasm difficulties in women.

- Question your physician about any prescription medication you may be taking. Some drugs can lead to impotence (in men) or a lessening of sexual desire (in both sexes). Tranquilizers and antidepressants sometimes fall into this category, as do some drugs used to control high blood pressure. The dosages of necessary medication can always be reduced to lessen these side effects.

- Cut down on coffee. Consider switching to herbal tea. Caffeine affects the entire nervous system, including sexual function.

In addition to these recommendations, I would add giving up smoking. One relatively underreported effect of smoking is that it can decrease the production of vaginal lubrication by a woman. This results in more painful and difficult intercourse.

Diet is also important in sexual physiology. Men who have higher levels of high-density lipoproteins (good cholesterol, or HDL) have lower incidences of impotence. Overeating should be avoided, as should very salty or heavily spiced foods.

An appropriate low-fat diet requires that no more than 20 percent of daily calories consumed are from fat. Many people state that fresh and lightly cooked lean meat (not pork) actually increases their sexual energy.

Affirmations and Beliefs for Sexual Bliss

Practice the following affirmations to facilitate your goal of attaining sexual bliss.

- *I am free of all past hurts and create a present and future path of sexual bliss.*

* *I am an empowered soul and have chosen a partner who is equally empowered.*

* *Both my partner and I support each other's identity, individuality, and independence. Our relationship balances out our respective energies and promotes spiritual growth.*

* *I am a quality soul and deserve all the advantages of a loving relationship characterized by sexual bliss.*

* *I accept the possibility of both pain and joy in my relationships, and I learn from both of them.*

A true form of sexual empowerment is depicted when you arrive at your own unique truth about yourself and intimate relationships. When you are willing to take complete responsibility for creating the path and direction of your life by determining what you value and want (not need), you have made great progress toward this empowerment.

Restructuring Sexual Beliefs

Self-hypnosis can be used to remove the following limiting beliefs dealing with sexuality and relationships:

Limiting Belief	Empowered Belief
• My own sexual pleasure is not as important as that of my partner.	• Sexual bliss encompasses mutual pleasure from lovemaking, and I deserve the right to give and receive this pleasure.
• My past hurtful relationships will continue on as "baggage."	• I create my own reality and let go of past scars and resentments.
• Successful sex requires reaching an orgasm.	
• Sex will eventually become boring and lack passion in a long-term relationship.	• My energy and spiritual growth will project a positive, clear message to all men or women I meet.
	• My commitment to my spiritual growth and openness will foster keeping our passion alive with the passage of time.

Now, I would like you to write down your limiting sexual beliefs, along with empowered solutions to these compromised notions. Practice the superconscious mind tap (see Chapter 10), and reprogram these limiting beliefs out of your awareness.

Overcoming Sexual Dysfunction

Many of my patients seek my hypnotherapy services to eliminate their sexual difficulties. Although the techniques and exercises presented in this section will work in a majority of cases, I highly recommend that anyone afflicted with severe sexual dysfunction enlist the services of a qualified professional.

Secondary impotence is the most common sexual dysfunction I treat. Primary impotence refers to the fact that the etiology of the sexual problem is entirely medical or organic. This is actually quite rare. Even Masters and Johnson reported less than 3 percent of their cases fit this category.[2]

Secondary impotence has a strong mental/emotional component and can occur in any age group from adolescence onward, though, naturally, the tendency to develop it increases with age. For some, it is intermittent in nature, whereas for others it is chronic. Some people arrive at the condition gradually; for others, it occurs quite literally overnight. No matter how it arrives, it is a disaster of the first magnitude for most men, and the stress and frustration that it can cause can be overwhelming.

Dealing With Impotence and Premature Ejaculation

This section presents techniques for overcoming sexual dysfunctions and paves the way for the attainment of sexual bliss. Practice the following script to overcome premature ejaculation and secondary impotence:

It will be easier and easier to be more relaxed and confident at each sexual experience. It is easier and easier to enjoy making love, excited yet relaxed. It is easy to last (maintain an erection) as long as you wish. You are getting more pleasure and enjoyment from making love every time. During intercourse, you are completely relaxed and uninhibited. You are steadily losing your susceptibility to be impotent and/or to prematurely ejaculate.

When you are making love, you are always relaxed and at ease. Your mind is filled with feelings of pleasure, causing you to act normally and naturally. Sex should not be regarded as a performance, but as an act from which both partners derive pleasure. So feelings of pleasure—of loving and being loved—saturate your mind, causing your behavior to be normal and natural. Sex is normal and natural. Enjoying sex is normal and natural.

Systematic Desensitization

Systematic desensitization uses the approach of creating hierarchies, whereby patients have gradually been conditioned to an anxiety situation, associated, for example, with sex, and learn to control this anxiety response through relaxation techniques. (This hierarchical approach was discussed in-depth in Chapter 3.)

With self-hypnosis the patient is trained to visualize anxiety-producing stimuli from the lower end of the hierarchy and to counter it with relaxation. This anxiety component of the hierarchy is eliminated through repetition of this procedure.

A patient of mine, a young male college student, exhibited severe anxiety reactions whenever he engaged in sex with his girlfriend. He created the following hierarchy:

1. Intercourse.
2. Sex play.
3. Intimate embrace.
4. Fondling.
5. Kissing.
6. Holding hands.
7. A movie date.
8. Having a conversation with his girlfriend alone.
9. Conversing with a group of his friends in which his girlfriend is included.

He was trained in self-hypnosis and given a conditioning tape to practice before our desensitization session. This technique is based on the principle that by presenting only mildly disturbing images beginning with the last item on the hierarchy, he is led to overcome his anxiety for each item. Each item is then presented in a graduated sequence until even the most anxiety-provoking image can be visualized with ease. It is important to use imagery that is familiar to each patient. This is why I have patients create the hierarchy.

Patients must be completely relaxed. They begin with the weakest stimulus and gradually proceed to the strongest. New items are introduced only when patients are able to picture preceding scenes without expressing anxiety.

Another method is to have patients produce a warm feeling in their hands and gradually transfer this sensation to the penis. Real-life situations that stimulate sexual desire can also be used.

A Self-Hypnosis Exercise

The following script illustrates this approach.

> *Just settle back as comfortably as you can. Let yourself relax to the very, very best of your ability. Imagine a warm and relaxing feeling spreading from the toes of your feet to the top of your head as I count backwards from 20 to one. Twenty, 19, 18, imagine this warm feeling moving up the body. Seventeen, 16, 15, 14, 13...this feeling is now permeating throughout the legs, hip, back, and chest. Twelve, 11, 10, nine, eight...spreading into the arms and neck. Seven, six, five, four, three...almost to the top of the head. Two and one. Now, each and every muscle of the body is completely relaxed.*

> *To further increase the relaxation, just for a moment, I would like you to tense all the muscles in your body, head pressed back against the chair, arms and fists clenched, toes pointed toward your face, creating tension along the backs of your legs. Tense all over, and now relax. Relax your entire body, and as you relax like that, let yourself go further all the time into a deep relaxed state, a deep relaxed state, all the time going further and further, further and further.*

> *I want you to imagine that you are standing at the top of a long escalator, and as you stand at the top of the escalator, safe*

and secure, watch the stairs go down further and further, going down and away. You let your eyes watch the stairs go down; as the stairs go down, you too go down; you too go down further and further into hypnosis. Calmly, safely, and securely. Now, you grasp the railings of the escalator and step off onto the first stair, riding the escalator down now, grasping the railings, grasping the railings calmly and securely. You go down further and further. As you go down the escalator, you go down further and further and further into hypnosis, a deep restful hypnotic trance. Going down deeper and further all the time, deeper and further all the time, a deep hypnotic rest. Going down deeper and deeper, all the way down deep. A good deep calm as your whole body relaxes, going down further and further, down all the way now.

Continue to imagine yourself riding the escalator down, and each time you exhale, your whole body becomes so much more comfortably heavy, so much more comfortably relaxed, so much more comfortably heavy and relaxed each time you breathe out. It helps you go deeper and deeper and deeper into hypnosis, a deep, restful hypnotic trance. As you continue to ride the escalator down, you go down further and further and further all the time now. So comfortably heavy and relaxed, enjoying the state of hypnosis.

Now, let the relaxation take you deeper and deeper into hypnosis all the time, a good, deep, restful hypnosis, as your whole body just eases up as you go down further and further all the time. In this comfortable, deep state of hypnosis, it will be very easy for you to respond to my instructions. What I want you to do is just to carry on relaxing.

Imagine that your right hand is becoming warmer and warmer. Just imagine the blood flowing freely to the very, very tip of your fingers, the blood flowing freely to the very, very tip of your fingers of your right hand. So comfortably relaxed all over as the blood flows freely to the very tips of your right hand. Your hand becomes warmer and warmer as this blood carries the warmth to the very, very tips of your fingers. A deeper and deeper level of hypnosis as you breathe freely and gently, going down deeper and deeper, each time letting your right hand become warmer, a very, very comfortable warmth, a good comfortable warmth as the rest of your body relaxes, letting the blood flow to the very, very tips of your right hand fingers. That's fine, just going down further and further now. That's just fine, the blood flowing to the very, very tips of your fingers. So comfortably relaxed, you may even notice a tingly feeling in the fingers. If this occurs, if this happens to you, just appreciate the feeling.

Continue relaxing like this all the time I am talking to you in hypnosis. Let your right hand become more and more comfortably warm, more and more comfortably at ease, comfortably warm as the blood flows to the very, very tips of the fingers of your right hand. Your left hand is now remaining as it was and your right hand becoming warmer. Your right hand is so comfortably warm as your whole body relaxes further and further.

Now, I want you to slowly move your right hand toward your penis and gently touch it. The warm feeling from your right hand is being transferred to your penis, allowing you to feel sexually excited. Your right hand is now the same temperature as your left hand, because it has returned to its normal state. Take a few moments and sense this exciting sexual feeling spreading through the entire genital region, including your penis.

PLAY NEW AGE MUSIC FOR FOUR MINUTES.

End your trance as usual.

Female Sexual Dysfunction

Medical screenings should always be initiated first to rule out organic causes of any sexual dysfunction. For example, a gynecological examination should rule out clitoral adhesions, which can prevent normal sexual function in a woman.

Female orgasmic disorder can be in a mild or severe form. Some women refuse to have anything to do with sex at all, whereas others will submit and get little out of it other than the knowledge that at least they have "done their duty" and kept their partners happy. Some women find that they have the desire and interest initially; however, once the act of sexual intercourse has begun, desire and interest fade, and what should be a pleasant and emotionally satisfying activity turns into a laborious chore. Many marriages fail for this very reason. A relationship based on sexual fulfillment alone has, at best, a rocky foundation. Learning the art of sexual bliss, however, brings other, more important dimensions into this relationship.

Using hypnosis to undergo age regression can uncover the source of fears and traumatic experiences that may have created this dysfunction. Proper use of self-hypnosis will result in an increasing awareness of a woman's own sexuality and greater participation in sexual activity. In most cases, the relationship between the woman and her partner will grow ever stronger. This creates a base from which sexual bliss can grow.

Negative self-suggestions throughout a woman's life can program her to accept orgasmic dysfunction as the norm. For example, the nonorgasmic woman whose sexual self-perception is negatively focused on her small breasts during her progression through the excitement phase may be more susceptible to orgasm dysfunction. If the woman's partner stimulates her breasts, she begins to repeat her well-practiced negative self-suggestions about her small breasts. Instead of this stimulation serving to help the woman reach the plateau phase, it either constitutes a distraction or results in her assuming a spectator role.

Any negative self-suggestion can reduce vasocongestion (blood flowing into the organ), thereby precluding advancement to the next sexual response stage or attenuating response in the present stage. The development of the spectator role—that is, thinking, "Oh, what am I doing wrong now? I shouldn't be concentrating on my small breasts; I should be really getting excited. Am I lubricating enough for him?"—was thought by Masters and Johnson to contribute to the inability of the female to reach orgasm.[3]

A Self-Hypnosis Exercise

A hypnotic script can be applied easily to build up the self-image. The self-confidence suggestions I presented in the male dysfunction section can be used as an introduction. After that, the following script can be added to facilitate more functional sexual responses in the woman.

You are getting more pleasure and enjoyment from making love every time. During intercourse, you are completely relaxed and uninhibited. It's easier and easier to enjoy intercourse, excited yet relaxed. It will be easier and easier to be more relaxed and confident at each sexual experience. You are steadily losing your susceptibility to be frigid.

Your lover is a good man, but he cannot help his critical attitude, because it is largely a result of his early training and upbringing. You will find yourself able to make allowances for him, and you will learn to ignore what you consider his criticisms. In fact, you will find the irritations and the annoyances of the situation rolling off you like water rolls off a duck's back. You are developing sufficient ego strength to become invulnerable to these annoyances. As a result, your sexual responses are returning to normal and you are functioning normally and naturally in that respect. Your vagina is becoming more lubricated as you think of making love, and when your partner is with you.

When you are making love, you are always relaxed and at ease. Your mind is imbued with feelings of pleasure, causing you to act normally and naturally. Sex should not be regarded as a performance, but as an act from which both partners derive pleasure. So feelings of pleasure—of loving and being loved—saturate your mind, causing your behavior to be normal and natural. Sex is normal and natural. Enjoying sex is normal and natural.

End your trance as usual.

I find it more productive for a patient to create his or her sexual hierarchy while in a hypnotic state.

One patient did just that, and she presented the following hierarchy:

1. Having intercourse in the nude while on husband's lap.
2. Having intercourse in the nude on top of bed.
3. Having intercourse in the nude under covers.
4. Vaginal intromission of husband's fingers.
5. Caressing husband's genitals.
6. Breasts being caressed, both with clothes and without.
7. Embracing while semiclothed, being aware of husband's erection.
8. Contacting of tongues while kissing.
9. Having buttocks and thighs caressed.
10. Husband kissing neck and ears.
11. Sitting on husband's lap.

12. Being kissed.
13. Dancing with and embracing husband fully clothed.

Sexual Bliss Through Hypnosis Exercises

The following script is designed for women.

Every day, in every way, you become more and more self confident. You project a very positive self-image. You can do whatever you desire.

You are, from this moment on, going to release all your fears and manifest your desires, especially in the attainment of sexual bliss.

You are a free and powerful being. You attract and incorporate sexual bliss in your life.

You are at peace with yourself and the universe. You feel balanced, peaceful, and harmonious.

Your mind will assist you in attaining sexual bliss. You have the power and ability to reach a state of sexual bliss.

You see what you want in your mind and begin to manifest this goal. Your visualizations become your reality. You hold a clear image and combine it with emotional desire.

You now activate new sexual pleasure centers, and you enjoy your body more and more every day. You always make time for sex. Your body performs perfectly during sex without your thinking about it.

It is okay to have exotic sexual fantasies. You openly discuss your sexual needs with your partner and encourage your partner to do the same.

You now let go of sexual pressure and expectations and enjoy your sexual experiences. Sex gets better and better for you. You are open to new sexual experiences with your lover. Your sexual desire and intensity are increasing. From now on, you will be able to achieve the most enjoyable orgasm you have ever experienced while making love. You respond to your partner openly and with the greatest of pleasure.

Before making love, you clear your mind of all other distracting thoughts and feelings and focus all your attention on experiencing the most enjoyable sexual response humanly possible. You are connected with your higher self during this sexual response, and now create the new reality of sexual bliss.

Every time you make love with your partner, you will find yourself becoming aware, gradually at first, of rays of white light reaching down to you, sparkling white light, a cone of that light, surrounding you now, growing brighter and brighter, sparkling and shimmering, warming you with its radiance. As it washes over you, surrounding your whole body, changing in appearance from one moment to the next, but always brilliantly white, cascading around you and sometimes appearing to you as a white light.

A wondrously beautiful white light, dazzling, all around you as your body moves into it, feeling your body beginning to merge with it, and feeling your body experience potent energies within. Now, focus your consciousness on your vagina. Wholly focused on your vagina, become aware of a pool of gently swirling but potentially extremely powerful energies there, stimulating you to feel good all over.

Focus on that pool and, at first, slowly notice that you can experience a tingling and then increasingly stronger sensations as you direct that energy to rise along your spine. And be aware now of its power growing and growing and feel it as it gains momentum, slowly, as it gains more force, as it rises.

Keep focused on this intensely pleasurable feeling with a mental image of your partner as you make mad, passionate love. Do this now.

PLAY NEW AGE MUSIC FOR THREE MINUTES.

Continue to visualize this nonstop, yet blissfully pleasurable love-making experience with your partner. You are soon going to experience the most intense and pleasurable orgasm humanly possible.

This tingly feeling in your vagina rises up your spine slowly and sends a surging signal to your brain. This erupts now into a force of white light that is so powerful that it triggers an intense vibration throughout your entire body from the vagina all the way up your backbone.

Direct this force along your spine, up and down, building these tensions until you explode into a magnificent orgasm. Do this now.

PLAY NEW AGE MUSIC FOR THREE MINUTES.

Feel yourself now sinking backward with it, this aura of white light back and down again, back down a cylinder, until down at the bottom only a small white flame is burning. And you arise out of that fire, and the fire is extinguished.

And become aware of your flesh, but it has changed—as if your body has passed through some kind of important catharsis of fire; as if your body has been made new by that experience; as if you have been given access to more vital energies and powers than your body could draw on before.

Relax now, even deeper in trance, retaining the afterglow of your pleasure, relaxing, drained of all tensions, and feeling yourself relaxing through your whole body.

PLAY NEW AGE MUSIC FOR ONE MINUTE.

All right now. Sleep and rest. You did very, very well. Listen very carefully. I'm going to count forward now from one to five. When I reach the count of five, you will return to normal consciousness. You will be able to remember everything you experienced and reexperienced. You'll feel very relaxed, refreshed, and you'll be able to do whatever you have planned for the rest of the day or evening. You'll feel very positive about what you've just experienced, and very motivated about your confidence and ability to practice this exercise again to experience sexual bliss.

All right now. One, very, very deep. Two, you're getting a little bit lighter. Three, you're getting much, much lighter. Four, very, very light. Five, awaken. Wide-awake and refreshed.

Men can use the following script to attain their level of sexual bliss:

Every time you make love with your partner, you will experience an awareness of energies. These pleasurable energies are becoming more intense, more charged, more and more intense, more intensely vibrant and energetic, becoming ecstatic for consciousness, moving into a realm in which awareness is entirely of blissful sensation. This is a completely fulfilling blissful sensation, that is also emotion, that is also knowing, and that fundamentally is just pure being.

You can easily achieve and maintain an erection. Your body now performs perfectly during sex. You now maintain an erection and delay ejaculation until you are ready to release. You accept the fact that you are a sexually virile man.

Now, mentally see yourself proceeding along a path in the jungle, not lost in the heavy, lush vegetation or concerned about the teeming wildlife of the jungle, but somehow knowing how to proceed, though you certainly have never been here before.

And you're going to come to a clearing, where a very powerful ritual involving chanting and drumming is being performed by primitive people. This is an extremely wild and elemental sexual rite.

You will perceive it first as a spectator, seeing the fire in the center of the clearing, the naked, glistening bodies dancing, heaving, and resonating to the evermore compelling beating of the drums, until your own body is throbbing with that beat. Soon you are caught up in the ritual, feeling in your body what those primitive people are doing. You are feeling just everything they are feeling, knowing everything they are knowing, as they dissolve the individual consciousness of the participants in the ritual, creating one collective consciousness.

And you will be totally drawn into that, becoming part of it, a part of the totality of this ritual experience. And you will have ample time to experience the entire ritual. And beginning now, you find yourself on the path to that ritual!

PLAY NEW AGE MUSIC FOR THREE MINUTES.

As you listen to this music, your entire body—from the toes of your feet to your penis, along your spine to the top of your head—builds up a pulsating and intense sense of stimulation and sensuality. You are becoming more and more intense, until those combined sensations have become so ecstatically and blissfully intense as to be almost unbearable. Now, keep focused on this intense feeling with a mental image of your partner as you make mad, passionate love. Do this now.

PLAY NEW AGE MUSIC FOR FOUR MINUTES.

And as you did before, you will experience the music with your entire body, you will be touched by it, only now you have learned a lot about responding, so that this experience will be vastly more intense than the earlier one. The sensations actually will be so extremely pleasurable as to be almost unbearable, almost unbearably sensuous and sensual, stimulating in you physical pleasure as great as any you ever have known and in duration far exceeding any pleasures you have known.

While you are experiencing this, it will be just pure experience, so you won't be thinking about it at all, but nonetheless you will be learning how great your body's capacity is for pleasure and how extended experientially the duration of pleasure can be. Do this now.

PLAY NEW AGE MUSIC FOR TWO MINUTES.

Relax now, relax for a while and go deeper, retaining the afterglow of your pleasure, but relaxing, drained of all tensions, and feeling yourself relaxing through your whole body.

PLAY NEW AGE MUSIC FOR ONE MINUTE.

End your trance as usual.

Final Thoughts

To greatly benefit from these approaches, I highly recommend regular practice. In addition, you will need to be patient because it requires more time in the beginning to master these exercises. Soon, you will find yourself moving step by step, at your own speed, to a style of lovemaking that will exceed your wildest dreams.

CHAPTER 9

HYPNOSIS
WITH CHILDREN

We are born with the ability to enter into self-hypnosis for seven hours daily. As children, we spontaneously enjoyed this gift of rich imagination and creativity. Many of you developed this skill and use it in your daily lives, while others misplaced their full creative imagination or lost the power to direct its use.

If one demographic exists in which hypnosis is universally effective, it is among children. Traditionally, children do not fear hypnosis, exhibit a natural trust, and have vivid imaginations. These qualities are ideal for hypnosis and help explain why children between the ages of 8 and 16 are the ideal hypnotic patients (though I have worked with children as young as 4).

Consider the following four requirements for successfully applying clinical hypnosis with children.

1. The child must trust the therapist or parent working with him or her. The child must feel that the therapist is more than simply an extension of the parent. If the child feels that the therapist is there for him or her, trust will be established.

2. The child must believe in his or her ability to attain specific goals. Some parents are infamous for discouraging their children by stating, "You will never amount to anything, You are stupid and lazy," and so forth. This pattern must cease immediately for the child to grow.

3. Hypnosis should be made fun and enjoyable. The use of games, puppets, or magic tricks can be incorporated into the session in a therapeutic manner. These techniques and others will make the sessions a pleasurable experience.

4. The child must desire the goal sought. A parent having a strong desire to see the child improve is not enough. A simple approach to encourage the child to improve is known as the add-on approach. For example, the child agrees to improve his or her grades in school, while at the same time being trained to improve his or her skills in sports (or some other desired goal). Subconsciously, the child associates the two areas of improvement with equal importance.

Examples of goals children can attain through the use of hypnosis are:

♦ Eliminating bed-wetting.
♦ Overcoming thumb-sucking.
♦ Improving grades.
♦ Eliminating phobias.
♦ Improving conduct.

Parents can use the scripts presented in this chapter with their children. It is preferable to make tapes of these exercises and supervise your child's use of them. If you do not wish to produce these yourself, feel free to contact my office for a list of professionally recorded tapes. I also have specially designed music for the recommended open spaces in the scripts.

It is important to encourage your child's growth on all levels. In general, children who demonstrate healthier relationships do better in life. If children can learn to solve their own problems, they are less likely to become aggressive, withdrawn, impulsive, antisocial, or insensitive. For example, overly withdrawn children often exhibit low self-esteem, depression, and loneliness as adults.

It is important for children to learn at an early age how to deal with problems and issues they experience in their interactions with others. The empowered child is more sensitive to the feelings of others and makes better choices throughout his or her life.

For example, the proper use of self-hypnosis can assist a child in:

- Properly evaluating whether an idea is wise.
- Seeking alternative solutions to a problem.
- Being sensitive to the effects of actions or choices on others.
- Functioning as a better role model for a younger sibling.
- Learning how to ask for help when overwhelmed by a situation.
- Properly assessing social signals from others.
- Raising self-image and becoming empowered.

It is equally important that parents refrain from pressuring their children by expecting too much too soon. This form of performance pressure can result in a child developing anxiety and a low self-image. On the other hand, children who become empowered develop health-coping skills and a stronger sense of their own competence and potential.

Children who are taught self-hypnosis experience an inner balance between what goes on in their inner-feeling world and the outside world of life around them. They are able to experience their own and other's inner worlds with understanding, rather than accusing others of being wrong or feeling that they are always being put down. This harmonizing of the inner life and the outer life leads to unity and oneness.

These children gain strength and sureness that they take with them and build on throughout life. Learning to be clear, and stay clear, enables children to develop a strong sense of social responsibility as they learn to extend this clarity to larger social problems.

A Self-Hypnosis Exercise

By changing any negative attitudes and lowered self-confidence levels, your children will eliminate the tendency to become discouraged or depressed about their lives. This will only function to ensure their ultimate success.

No amount of willpower can surmount this feeling of defeatism. Your child absolutely must develop feelings of self-esteem and confidence in order to become empowered.

Any negative thoughts will filter into your child's subconscious mind, which does not question or analyze the data it receives. A child's self-image determines, to a large degree, how the child goes about solving problems. If children have experienced repeated failure in past attempts to change a behavior pattern, their total self-image becomes established and fixed as one of failure.

They now become so convinced that they are incapable of reversing this trend that they eventually stop mentally picturing a desirable goal for themselves. Your children now resign themselves to accept their current situation as being permanent and helpless.

A positive self-image must be fed into their subconscious mind without being evaluated by the critical factor of their conscious mind proper (defense mechanisms). The most efficient and effective method of accomplishing this goal is by practicing self-hypnosis.

By mentally seeing themselves as they desire to be, your children are reprogramming their subconscious computer. This does not require a critical acceptance, as their subconscious is incapable of analytical thought. Accompanying this visualization will be a feeling that they have already attained this goal. This "as if" approach is remarkably successful.

Once they achieve a particular goal using their subconscious mind, the maintenance of this goal will now be effortless. When something attempts to interfere with the proper functioning of the now reprogrammed subconscious, their internal computer will recognize this error immediately, and it will be corrected by this feedback mechanism.

Your children's initial efforts in reprogramming their subconscious will require a certain amount of mental mind set, which will encompass all their new goals and aspirations. Daily practice of the exercises presented in this chapter will result in a permanent reprogramming of their subconscious computer, and a spontaneous incorporation of this goal. Willpower is neither necessary nor desirable for this paradigm. This is one example of raising consciousness.

Your children's imagination must create a new mental image of themselves. If they have properly implanted their subconscious with positive images and suggestions, they automatically alter their behavior to act in accord with this new programming. A new sense of well-being and accomplishment will accompany this pattern of behavior. They will be able to feel this sense of confidence and psychic empowerment for prolonged periods following additional practice sessions.

Willpower alone cannot result in permanent changes in behavior. If it could you would not be reading this book. The problem with the willpower approach is that you are consciously placing too much emphasis on past failures. As a result, your mental mind set is not conducive to improvement, and subsequent efforts prove only more frustrating.

Success in applying consciousness-raising techniques to your children depends upon their subconscious mind's uncritical acceptance of constructive suggestions. I have found the best method of achieving this is by the use of self-hypnosis. This will function to quiet a child's mind. Children must incorporate quiet and relaxation into their lives if they are to raise their consciousness and become empowered.

Relaxation Awareness Exercises

A simple way to begin this relaxation approach is to ask your children to focus all their attention on the outside world. They now select one sound or smell with their eyes closed and say to themselves, "I am aware of _____." Next they shift their attention to their internal world of physical sensations and feelings. They say to themselves, "I am now aware of _____." They will most commonly observe that the previous external awareness is now replaced by their inner focus.

As another exercise, have your children sit or lie down and let their minds scan their bodies with their eyes closed. Ask them to observe any sensations, from their breathing to their stomach's gurgling, without judging them. During this body scan, instruct them to pause for a moment at each body part or organ.

Your child is to note any tenseness, and begin to use affirmations to suggest relaxation in these tense muscles. Allow at least 5 minutes for this exercise, and have the child repeat it several times during the next week.

There are many activities children enjoy, and that can facilitate a state of relaxation. Some examples are:

- ◆ Observing the clouds.
- ◆ Viewing a funny movie or television show.
- ◆ Playing with their pet.
- ◆ Taking a relaxing walk.
- ◆ Doing some arts and crafts.
- ◆ Going to the ocean or a park.
- ◆ Mentally recalling a favorite vacation.

When training children to use self-hypnosis, always communicate at their intellectual level. It is helpful to make this technique fun, as in playing a game. I commonly use a TV program technique with young children. By having them play a role in the show, they are more interested in the results and feel more in control of the situation.

Here is a sample TV program exercise for phobia elimination.

Imagine yourself sitting in front of your television and watching yourself as the star of a program. You see yourself going through a typical day in your life and are exposed several times to the very things that make you scared. The difference is that now you are calm and you no longer have these fears.

Take a few moments and see these scenes of yourself free of discomforts and happy. Do this now.

PLAY NEW AGE MUSIC FOR THREE MINUTES.

You no longer have these fears and feel good about yourself in every way.

Children between the ages of 8 and 16 make the best hypnotic patients. Your child will find these techniques both fun and empowering.

Focused Concentration and Study Improvement— A Self-Hypnosis Exercise

Any child can be trained to focus his or her concentration by performing simple mental calculations for 20 minutes a day during a period of three weeks. Try this simple exercise.

Take a deep breath, fill your chest, and hold it until I tell you to let go. I am going to count slowly up to five, and as I do so, you will take five very deep breaths. And with each deep breath that you take, each time you breathe out, you will become more and more and more relaxed, and your trance will become deeper and deeper.

One, breathe deeply, more and more deeply relaxed, deeper and deeper into relaxation. Two, breathe deeper, deeper and deeper becoming more relaxed, going deeper and deeper in hypnosis. Three, breathing even more deeply, more and more deeply relaxed, more and more deeply relaxed. Four, more and more deeply relaxed, deeper and deeper relaxed, your trance depth is becoming even deeper and deeper. Five, very, very deep breath, very, very deeply relaxed, very, very deeply relaxed.

Once again, I want you to take one very deep breath, fill your chest and hold it until I say let go. Then, let your breath out as quickly as possible, and as you do so, you will feel yourself sagging limply back into the chair, and you will become twice as deeply relaxed as you are now, twice as deeply relaxed. Now, take that very deep breath and fill your chest. Hold it (10 second pause); hold it (10 second pause); hold it (10 second pause). Let go.

Now, mentally recite the addition table in your mind, starting with one plus one equals two, and going methodically through each number up to one plus nine equals 10. Then, continue with two plus one equals three, and so on, until you have recited all the sums up to nine plus nine equals 18. Keep your attention closely focused on the mental task and notice when you start to wander from it. Return to the beginning and start again if your concentration wanders. Following the successful completion of this phase, switch to the multiplication table for variety.

End your trance as usual, or simply open your eyes.

For a more advanced method in training your child for mindfulness, have him or her remain in the trance, allowing his or her mind to wander (on any subject) for about one minute. Then, instruct the child to focus on a specific school assignment. Reflect on the end result you want him or her to achieve and the benefits of getting it done.

Now, select one of the more interesting features of the task, and use this item to hook the child's attention more closely into the task. Gradually, narrow his or her attention to the subject at hand and move toward the beginning of the task you have set. Instruct the child to keep his or her attention focused on the goal as he or she proceeds. Monitor the child's progress and repeat this technique from the original starting point if his or her concentration breaks down.

Memory Improvement for Exams

Children have a natural ability to visualize, and we can use this talent to assist them with improving their memory.

A Self-Hypnosis Exercise

The following script can be used to improve memory.

You have an excellent memory and are now going to use it to do well on your test. As you practice this exercise, your memory is improving steadily every day. You can easily recall everything you read with ease.

As you enter the examination room, you feel confident, relaxed, and calm. When you read the questions, your memory is immediately activated and your mind is filled with the information that will allow you to answer the questions correctly.

You will find that by saying "20, 20, 20" you will quickly and deeply place yourself into a deep hypnotic trance, and then you may ask your subconscious directly for information on answering any question. Then, continue with the questions you can answer easily, and you will find that the answers to the more difficult questions simply pop into your mind.

Now, take a few moments and see yourself in class getting your exam back. You received an A, and the teacher is telling you how proud he or she is of your improvement and performance on this test. Also focus on how good you feel knowing that you prepared well and showed your knowledge on this test. Do this now.

PLAY NEW AGE MUSIC FOR THREE MINUTES.

End this trance as usual.

Hole-in-the-Top-of-Head Technique

Here is another visualizing method that children find fun and easy to do.

Have your child pretend that he has a hole in the top of his head so when looking directly upward he can see the ceiling of the room, or sky if outdoors.

Next, instruct him to look through the top of his head at the ceiling and tell him that his eyelids are now glued shut so he cannot open them. When he tries to look up at the ceiling through this imaginary hole in the top of his head, he will find it physically impossible to open his eyes.

Because it is physically impossible to open our eyes when the eyeballs are turned upward, this method fosters further cooperation and eliminates resistance to hypnosis.

Thumb-Sucking

Thumb-sucking usually subsides by the age of 4 in most children. Some children return to this habit as a pacifier when they are tired, sleepy, bored, or hungry.

A Self-Hypnosis Exercise

Try the following blackboard exercise to eliminate thumb-sucking.

Imagine yourself in your classroom going up to the blackboard. You see the following statement on the board.

I am a thumb-sucker.

Now, take the eraser and erase this statement. From now on, you will no longer suck your thumb. You are never going to suck your thumb again.

Here is another exercise to eliminate thumb-sucking.

I know your parents want you to stop sucking your thumb, but that doesn't seem fair, does it? I believe we should always be fair, don't you?

I see no reason why you can't suck your thumb as long as you are fair. Don't you agree? To be fair, each one of your fingers should be sucked if you are going to suck your thumb. Isn't that fair?

From now on, whenever you suck your thumb, you are going to suck each of your other fingers for the same amount of time. If you do not do that, you can no longer suck your thumb because that would not be fair, would it?

Bed-Wetting

Bed-wetting is often a sign that a child is stressed. Hypnosis can quickly rid a child of this unwanted habit.

A Self-Hypnosis Exercise

The following script will aid in eliminating bed-wetting.

I want you to pretend that you are watching your favorite television program at home. Pick up the remote control and change the channel to a show that stars you.

See yourself throughout the day having breakfast, going off to school, playing with your friends, having dinner with your family, and so forth. Imagine yourself being happy and confident.

Notice that you never have anything to drink before bedtime and that you always remember to go to the bathroom immediately before you get into bed. You are not worried about whether or not your bed will be dry the following morning.

See yourself waking up in the middle of the night if you have to go to the bathroom and returning to bed after you use the toilet. Now, see yourself waking up in the morning in a dry bed and being rewarded by your parents for being so good. Do this now.

PLAY NEW AGE MUSIC FOR THREE MINUTES.

End the trance as usual.

Disobedience

Children often use unruly behavior as attention-getting devices. Rebellious behavior suggests that a child is angry and does not fear punishment or loss of love from his or her parents.

A Self-Hypnosis Exercise

The following script will help correct a disobedient child.

Imagine yourself sitting in front of your television and watching yourself being the star of the show. This episode deals with your behavior. First, take a few moments and see yourself acting in ways that make your parents angry. Do this now.

PLAY NEW AGE MUSIC FOR THREE MINUTES.

Now, see yourself asking for a treat, such as going to an amusement park or the beach, or getting an ice cream sundae. Your parents tell you that because of your behavior you will not receive this treat. They punish you by sending you to your room without dinner, and taking away your television set for an entire week.

Now, see yourself eliminating the very behaviors that make your parents angry and see how happy they are. Also, see yourself being rewarded with all kinds of fun treats. See how enjoyable this is. Do this now.

PLAY NEW AGE MUSIC FOR THREE MINUTES.

From now on, you are going to behave as you just saw on television, and never again will you misbehave and make your parents mad. End your trance as usual.

Final Thoughts

It is my thesis that children want to grow in every way and be all they can be. With proper motivation and simple relaxation techniques, any goal is attainable. Consciousness raising is as natural as breathing, using the methods presented in this chapter. Children as young as 5 can apply these procedures.

The steps that children (and parents) can take to raise their consciousness and empower themselves may be summarized as follows:

- Practice self-hypnosis daily by using any of the techniques presented in this chapter.
- Reprogram your child's subconscious by direct suggestions and visual imagery to build up self-image and confidence levels.
- Program solutions to your child's everyday problems and acceptable behavior by daily use of self-hypnosis.
- Continue practice sessions after initial success to avoid terminating this training prematurely.

As parents you can gradually phase out these techniques as your child becomes more empowered and eliminates negative behaviors.

CHAPTER 10

NEW AGE HYPNOSIS

Spirituality has been receiving increased attention from both healthcare providers and consumers. Spirit is understood to be both the source and a manifestation of one's spirituality. Spirituality is a unifying force, manifested in the self and reflected in one's being, one's knowing, and one's doing. It is expressed and experienced in the context of caring connections with oneself, others, nature, the Higher Self (the perfect component of our souls or subconscious minds), and God.

The key elements of this view of spirituality are the self and connections. The self reflects an unfolding life journey that embodies who one is, what and how one knows, and what one does, as well as one's source of strength and meaning. Connections are those attachments and relationships that link the self to others, nature, the Higher Self, and God. Spirituality relates to an inner knowing and source of strength reflected in one's being, one's knowing, and one's doing. Hypnosis can be used to establish a link between the subconscious (soul) and the Higher Self (superconscious mind) to raise consciousness. This is my definition of New Age hypnosis.

Superconscious Mind Tap

One method that is extraordinarily effective in eliminating problems is a technique that I developed in 1977, known as the *superconscious mind tap*. The basis for this technique is to raise the quality of the subconscious mind's energy.

A component of the subconscious is perfect, and it is called the *superconscious mind*, or *Higher Self*. By introducing the subconscious mind to its perfect counterpart (the superconscious) through self-hypnosis, the quality of the energy (electromagnetic radiation) that comprises the subconscious can be raised. I call this technique *cleansing*. (A thorough discussion of cleansing is presented in my book *Soul Healing*.)

A Self-Hypnosis Exercise

The following script can be used to train yourself in the art of accessing your Higher Self for the purpose of resolving any troublesome issue.

Now listen very carefully. I want you to imagine a bright white light coming down from above and entering the top of your head, filling your entire body. See it, feel it, and it becomes reality. Now, imagine an aura of pure white light emanating from your heart region, again surrounding your entire body, protecting you. See it, feel it, and it becomes reality. Now, only your Higher Self, masters and guides, and highly evolved loving entities who mean you well will be able to influence you during this or any other hypnotic session. You are totally protected by this aura of pure white light.

In a few moments, I am going to count from one to 20. As I do so, you will feel yourself rising up to the superconscious mind level at which you will be able to access your Higher Self and both explore and remove the causes of _____. One, rising up. Two, three, four, rising higher. Five, six, seven, letting information flow. Eight, nine, 10, you are halfway there. Eleven, 12, 13, feel yourself rising even higher. Fourteen 15, 16, almost there. Seventeen, 18, 19, number 20. Now you are there. Take a moment and orient yourself to the superconscious mind level.

PLAY NEW AGE MUSIC FOR ONE MINUTE.

You are now in a deep hypnotic trance, and from this superconscious mind level there exists a complete understanding and resolution of _____. You are in complete control and able to access this limitless power of your superconscious mind. I want you to be open and flow with this experience. You are always protected by the white light.

At this time, I would like you to ask your Higher Self to explore the origin of your _____. Trust your Higher Self and your own ability to allow any thoughts, feelings, or impressions to come into your subconscious mind concerning this goal. Do this now.

PLAY NEW AGE MUSIC FOR THREE MINUTES.

Now, I would like you to let go of the situation, regardless of how simple or complicated it may seem. Allow your Higher Self to facilitate the raising of your soul's energy to the level well above having any form of _____.

At this time, I want you to see yourself in your current awareness free of _____ and visualize yourself completely cured. Do this now.

PLAY NEW AGE MUSIC FOR FOUR MINUTES.

You have done very well. Now, I want you to further open up the channels of communication by removing any obstacles and allowing yourself to access information and experiences that will directly apply to and help better your present awareness. Allow yourself to receive more advanced and more specific information from your Higher Self to raise your soul's energy and remove _____ and any other problems from your awareness. Do this now.

PLAY NEW AGE MUSIC FOR FOUR MINUTES.

All right. Sleep now and rest. You have done very, very well. Listen very carefully. I'm going to count forward now from one to five. When I reach the count of five, you will be back in your current conscious awareness. You will be able to remember everything you experienced.

You'll feel very relaxed and refreshed, and you'll be able to do whatever you have planned for the rest of the day or evening. You'll feel very positive about what you've just experienced and very motivated about your confidence and ability to play this tape again to experience your Higher Self.

All right now. One, very, very, very deep. Two, you're getting a little bit lighter. Three, you're getting much, much lighter. Four, very, very light. Five, awaken. Wide-awake and refreshed.

This technique forms the basis of my approach to training my patients to take charge of their lives and grow spiritually. I refer to this as *psychic empowerment*.

Reincarnation

A core New Age concept is the belief in reincarnation, or the soul occupying a new body after the physical death of the previous one. To a skeptic, there can be no consciousness after the physical body dies. The universe is composed exclusively of material realities, and without the physical organism there can be no mind, no consciousness, and certainly no life after death. Near-death experiences are but hallucinations caused by reasons that may be psychological, pharmacological, or neurological. It may be impossible for such a thing as objective proof to ever actually exist in matters of the mind and spirit. Interestingly, a recent Gallup poll showed that 58 percent of Americans believe in reincarnation.[1]

I have conducted more than 35,000 individual past-life regressions and future-life progressions on more than 12,000 individual patients. I can attest to the relative ease with which anyone, with a little assistance from hypnosis, can tap into these lifetimes.

Jerry Springer's Past Life

The term *healthy skeptic* best describes Jerry Springer's attitude toward past-life regression. As part of an interview I did with him, Jerry was guided back into one of his previous lifetimes. This show aired January 7, 1994, and Jerry reran his taped past-life experience in October of that year.

As a knight in England during the 1600s, Jerry was severely wounded in a battle defending the honor of a noblewoman. He could no longer function as a knight, so the woman he saved employed him in the castle as a butler. This woman reincarnated as Jerry's current-life daughter. This is a case of karmic family values.

A Past-Life Case Becomes a TV Movie

My most dynamic case of past-life regression is reported in my book, *The Search for Grace: The True Story of Murder and Reincarnation.* The patient, whom I shall call Ivy, was obsessively attracted to John. Although John attempted to murder Ivy on three separate occasions, she was unable to break away from this relationship. The soul of John had murdered Ivy in 20 of her 46 past lives uncovered during hypnosis. She wanted desperately to break off the relationship and end the recurrent nightmares from which she awoke screaming in terror every night—being murdered repeatedly by the same mysterious man—but she just couldn't seem to pull herself free.

Ivy reported the following facts to me during hypnosis. She lived in Buffalo, N.Y., during the 1920s as a woman named Grace Doze. She was a cold and calculating woman who had little respect for her husband, Chester, whom she held in contempt. Grace had many affairs during her marriage. She was a real Roaring Twenties party girl. Grace was responsible enough not to abandon her son, Cliff, but, beyond that concession to maturity, her lifestyle was hedonistic.

One evening, in early May of 1927, Grace met a bootlegger named Jake at a speakeasy. They saw quite a bit of each other during the next two weeks. She decided to leave Chester and move in with Jake, who had rented an apartment on Purdy Street. This event was to occur immediately following Grace's regular Tuesday night swimming session at the local high school on May 17.

When Jake picked up Grace on that fateful evening at about 9:45 p.m., he was drunk. When Grace mentioned that her son, Cliff, would be living with them, Jake became abusive. He was quick to anger, even when he wasn't drinking, and, as they drove, their discussion rapidly escalated into a heated argument. Without warning, Jake pulled the car off the road and punched Grace with his right hand. She was conscious, but in pain. Jake then strangled her until she died. CBS aired this case as a television movie on May 17, 1994, exactly 67 years to the hour since Grace Doze was murdered.

Ivy gave me more than two dozen facts that were verified by an independent researcher. She was finally able to break this karmic bond and go on with her life. Her case illustrates many aspects of soul healing. In addition to overcoming her obsession with John, she improved her self-image, overcame her fear of choking, and became an empowered soul. She took control of her life and is a happier person today as a result of her energy-cleansing experiences.

New Age techniques allow you to expand and explore your awareness and eliminate fear, anxiety, depression, and other negative tendencies, as well as the fear of death. New Age hypnosis is neither magic nor a panacea—it is a way to help shape the future. By creating your own reality with the knowledge from your subconscious and superconscious minds, you can positively affect your present and future lives.

The soul always has free will. We can choose to do good or evil, right or wrong. We choose our future lives. Who would choose to kill, rape, steal, or cheat if he or she realized the karmic implications? By learning to use these principles to better ourselves, we are bettering the future for all. The universe is connected to our souls by a linkage of the consciousness of all souls (the Higher Self). If we purposely do something good or bad, the universe will note this action and treat us accordingly.

The reincarnation process will end when you fulfill your karma. When you learn all the lessons you need to learn and show kindness and unselfish love to all those with whom you come into contact, the cycle will end. When it ends, you will go beyond the soul plane to the higher planes and reunite with God.

A Self-Hypnosis Exercise

Practice the following script to view one or more of your own past lives.

Now listen very carefully. I want you to imagine a bright white light coming down from above and entering the top of your head, filling your entire body. See it, feel it, and it becomes reality. Now, imagine an aura of pure white light emanating from the region surrounding your heart. Again surrounding your entire body, protecting you. See it, feel it, and it becomes reality.

Now, only your masters and guides and highly evolved loving entities who mean you well will be able to influence you during this or any other hypnotic session. You are totally protected by this aura of pure white light. Now listen very carefully. In a few minutes, I'm going to be counting backward from 20 to one. As I count backward from 20 to one, you are going to perceive yourself moving through a very deep and dark tunnel. The tunnel will get lighter and lighter, and at the very end of this tunnel, there will be a door with a bright white light above it. When you walk through this door, you will be in a past-life scene.

You're going to reexperience one of your past lives at the age of about 15. You'll be moving to an event that will be significant in explaining who you are, where you are, and why you are there. I want you to realize that if, at any time, you feel uncomfortable— physically, mentally, or emotionally—you can awaken yourself from this hypnotic trance by simply counting forward from one to five.

You will always associate my voice as a friendly voice in trance. You will be able to let your mind review its memory bank and follow the instructions of perceiving the scenes of your own past lives and following along as I instruct. You'll find yourself being able to get deeper and quicker in hypnotic trances each time as you practice with this tape or other methods of self-hypnosis. When you hear me say the words, "Sleep now and rest," I want you to immediately detach yourself from any scene you are experiencing. You will be able to await further instructions.

You absolutely have the power and ability to go back into a past life as your subconscious mind's memory bank remembers everything you've ever experienced in all your past lives as well as your present life. I want you to relive these past-life events as a neutral observer (without feeling or emotion), just as if you were watching a television show.

I want you to choose a past life now in which you've lived to at least the age of 30. I want you to pick a positive or neutral past-life experience. I'm going to count backward now from 20 to one. As I do so, I want you to feel yourself moving into the past. You'll find yourself moving through a pitch-black tunnel that will get lighter and lighter as I count backward. When I reach the count of one, you will have opened up a door with a bright white light above it and walked into a past-life scene.

You will once again become yourself at about the age of 15 in a previous lifetime. Now listen carefully. Number 20, you're moving into a very deep, dark tunnel surrounded by grass and trees and your favorite flowers and it is very, very inviting as you feel very calm and comfortable about moving into the tunnel. Nineteen, 18, you're moving backward in time, back, back, 17, 16, 15, the tunnel is becoming lighter now. You can make out your arms and legs, and you realize that you are walking through this tunnel and you're moving backward in time. Fourteen, 13, 12, moving so far back, back, back, 11, 10, nine, you're now so far back, you're more than halfway there, the tunnel is much lighter. You can see around you, and you can now make out the door in front of you with the bright white light above it. Eight, seven, six, standing in front of the door now feeling comfortable and feeling positive and confident about your ability to move into this past-life scene. Five, four, up to the door, put your hand on the doorknob, the bright white light is so bright it's hard to look at. Three, open the door; two, step through the door; one, move into the past-life scene.

Focus carefully on what you perceive before you. Take a few minutes now to let everything become crystal clear. The information flowing into your awareness, the scene is becoming visual and visible. Just let yourself become oriented to your new environment. Focus on it. Take a few moments to listen to my instructions.

Let the impression form. First, what do you see and what are you doing? Are you male or female? Look at your feet first—what type of footwear are you wearing? Now, move up the body and see exactly how you are clothed. How are you dressed? How old are you? What are you doing right now? What is happening around you?

Be able to describe the situation you find yourself in. Are you outdoors or indoors? Is it day or night? Is it hot or cold? What country or land do you live in or are you from? Now, focus on this one carefully—what do people call you? What is the year? Take a few moments, numbers may appear right in front of you. You will be informed of exactly what year this is. Take a few more moments and let any additional information crystallize and become clear in your awareness about the environment that you find yourself in, as well as yourself. Take a few moments. Let any additional information be made clear to you.

PLAY NEW AGE MUSIC FOR THREE MINUTES.

Very good now. Listen very carefully to my voice. Sleep now and rest. Detach yourself from this scene just for a moment. I'm going to be counting forward from one to five. When I reach the count of five, you're going to be moving forward now to a significant event that's going to occur in this lifetime that will affect you personally. It will also most probably affect those close to you— it may involve your parents, friends, people who are close to you in this lifetime. I want you to move forward to a significant event, but it's also going to be a positive one. It's going to be a positive event.

Focus carefully. Sleep now and rest and listen as I count forward in time to a significant positive event that is going to occur to you. One, moving forward, slowly, carefully, comfortably; two, feeling good as you move forward in time; three, halfway there; four, almost there; five.

Now, again focus on yourself and the environment you find yourself in. What are you doing now and why are you in this environment? Has anything changed since I last spoke with you? What is happening around you? Are there any other people around you who are important to you? If there are, are they male or female? Are they friends or relatives? How do they relate to you? Why are they important to you? Focus on your clothes now starting with your feet first. How are you dressed? Are you dressed any differently than when I last spoke with you? Move all the way up your body and perceive how you are dressed. Then, look at the people next to you; are they dressed any differently? About how old are you now? Focus on that for a moment—a number will appear to you—about how old are you right now?

Where exactly are you? Are you outdoors or indoors? Is it day or night? What season is this? What kind of occupation do you have? What do you do to pass the time? What do you do with your day? Focus on how you spend your time.

Now, I want you to focus on an event that's going to be happening right now—that you find yourself right in the middle of—I want you to spend a few moments and whatever this event is, I want you to carry it through to completion. This will be a positive or happy event only. Take a few moments and carry this event through to completion.

PLAY NEW AGE MUSIC FOR THREE MINUTES.

All right. Sleep now and rest. Detach yourself from this scene that you are experiencing and listen to my voice again. You're going to be moving forward now by a period of a minimum of three years. It can be as long as necessary, but a minimum of three years. You will not have died nor undergone any traumatic episode. It will be at least three years further in time.

Now, I want you to move forward to a significant event that is going to affect not only the kind of work that you do but also you personally. Affect the way you relate to certain people—people who are close to you perhaps—and certain goals that you have. I want you to move forward to this very significant time that is going to be positive or neutral, and it will be at least three years from now.

On the count of five, move forward very carefully and comfortably. One, moving forward; two, moving further forward; three, halfway there; four, almost there; five. Now focus on what you perceive around you. What has transpired since I last saw you? Focus on yourself first. Perceive where you are, how you are dressed, what environment you are in, where you are located (if it is a different physical environment), and who is with you. Take a few moments to let this information crystallize and become clear in your awareness.

PLAY NEW AGE MUSIC FOR THREE MINUTES.

All right. Sleep now and rest. Detach yourself from this scene. We're going to be moving forward again on the count of five. This time, you're going to be moving forward to a scene that is going to signify or illustrate the maximum achievements that you accomplished during this lifetime. This scene will illustrate the maximum accomplishments personally or professionally. You'll be surrounded by the people who affect you most in this lifetime. On the count of five, move forward to this maximum accomplishment during this lifetime. One, moving forward slowly, carefully, comfortably; two, moving further forward; three, halfway there; four, almost there; five.

Now, take a few moments and see where you find yourself. What is your environment? What has happened and why is this time of your life so important to you? Focus on it and see what you've accomplished, and let all the information be made clear to you.

PLAY NEW AGE MUSIC FOR THREE MINUTES.

Now that you've been able to perceive this particular period of your life, I want you to be able to evaluate it. I want you to find out what goals you were supposed to accomplish and what you actually did accomplish. What do you feel that you learned from this lifetime? What do you feel that you have gained from this lifetime—in your own personal goals, family life, and relationships? Let the information flow—what did you gain?

Now, let's focus on what you weren't able to achieve. Focus on what you felt you would have liked more time to accomplish. What do you feel that you just weren't able to accomplish and why? Focus on that. Let the information flow.

Now remember, in this particular lifetime you are still alive. I want you to focus on your activities, whatever you're involved in within this particular scene, to evaluate why this lifetime was important to you. What necessary or needed experience did you gain from this lifetime? Focus on this now. Let the information flow into your awareness.

PLAY NEW AGE MUSIC FOR THREE MINUTES.

All right. Sleep now and rest. You did very, very well. Listen very carefully. I'm going to count forward now from one to five, one more time. This time, when I reach five, you will be back in the present. You will be able to remember everything you experienced and reexperienced, you'll feel very relaxed, refreshed, and you'll be able to do whatever you have planned for the rest of the day or evening.

You'll feel very positive about what you've just experienced, and very motivated about your confidence and ability to play this tape again to experience additional lifetimes. All right now. One, very, very deep; two, you're getting a little bit lighter; three, you're getting much much lighter; four, very, very light; five, awaken. Wide-awake and refreshed.

Progression

In 1977, I developed the technique of guiding my patients into the future. I refer to this as *age progression* (going into the future of your current life) and *future-life* progression (viewing lives to be lived in centuries to come).

Jerry Springer's future life illustrates how this approach can explain the origin of a long-standing phobia. During the later part of the 21st century, Jerry will be a rancher/farmer named Bobby, working in Montana. He is married and has four children. Bobby is involved with a government project designed to raise crops on our moon. He will be killed at the age of 60 when his craft crashes during a return trip to Earth.

Two interesting facts surfaced from this future-life progression. First, Jerry's future-life wife is a girl he knew in high school named Robin. Second, he stated on his show that to this day he is afraid to dive into a pool. This phobia has led to much embarrassment during past vacations.

A Self-Hypnosis Exercise

Practice the following exercise to get a sneak preview of one of your future lives.

> *Now listen very carefully. I want you to imagine a bright white light coming down from above and entering the top of your head, filling your entire body. See it, feel it, and it becomes reality. Now, imagine an aura of pure white light emanating from the region surrounding your heart. Again surrounding your entire body, protecting you. See it, feel it, and it becomes reality. Now, only your masters and guides and highly evolved, loving entities who mean you well will be able to influence you during this, or any other, hypnotic session. You are totally protected by this aura of pure white light. Focus carefully on my voice as your subconscious mind's memory bank has memories of all past, present, and future lifetimes. This tape will help guide you*

into the future, the future of this life, or the future of another lifetime.

Soon, I am going to be counting forward from one to 20. As I count forward from one to 20, you are going to imagine yourself moving through a tunnel. Near the end of this count, you will perceive the tunnel veer off to the left and to the right—the right represents the past, the left represents the future. You're going to bear left. You're going to go through the left tunnel and this will take you into the future. On the count of 20, you will perceive yourself in the future. Your subconscious and superconscious mind levels have all the knowledge and information that you desire. Carefully and comfortably feel yourself moving into the future with each count from one to 20. Listen carefully now. Number one, feel yourself now moving forward to the future, into this very, very deep and dark tunnel. Two, three, farther and farther into the future. Four, five, six, the tunnel is very, very dark. It is a little bit disorienting, but you know you're moving into the future. Seven, eight, nine, it's more stable now and you feel comfortable, you feel almost as if you're floating, as if you're rising up and into the future.

Ten, 11, 12, the tunnel is now getting a little bit lighter and you can perceive a light at the end, another white light just like the white light that is surrounding you. Thirteen, 14, 15. Now you are almost there. Focus carefully. You can perceive a door in front of you, in this left tunnel that you are in now. The door will be opened in just a few moments, and you will see yourself in the future. The words "sleep now and rest" will always detach you from any scene you are experiencing and allow you to await further instructions. Sixteen, 17. It's very bright now, and you are putting your hands on the door. Eighteen, you open the door; 19, you step into this future, to this future scene. Number 20. Carefully focus on your surroundings, look around you, see what you perceive. Can you perceive yourself? Can you perceive other people around you? Focus on the environment. What does it look like? Carefully focus on this. Use your complete objectivity. Block out any information from the past that might have interfered with the quality of the scene.

Use only what your subconscious and superconscious mind level will observe. Now, take a few moments, focus carefully on the scene, find out where you are, what you are doing, why you are there. Take a few moments, let the scene manifest itself.

PLAY NEW AGE MUSIC FOR THREE MINUTES.

Now, focus very carefully on what year this is. Think for a moment. Numbers will appear before your inner eyes. You will have knowledge of the year that you are in right now. Carefully focus on this year and these numbers. They will appear before you. Use this as an example of other information that you are going to obtain. I want you to perceive this scene completely, carry it through to completion.

I want you to perceive exactly where you are, who you are, the name, the date, the place. I want you to carry these scenes to completion, follow them through carefully for the next few moments. The scene will become clear, and you will perceive the sequence of what exactly is happening to you.

PLAY NEW AGE MUSIC FOR THREE MINUTES.

You've done very well. Now, you are going to move to another event. I want you to focus on a different experience in the same future time. Perceive what is going on and why this is important to you. Perceive the year, the environment, the presence of others. Let the information flow.

PLAY NEW AGE MUSIC FOR THREE MINUTES.

As you perceive the details of the next scene, focus also on your purpose—your purpose in this future time and how it is affecting your karmic subcycle. Focus in on what you are learning, what you are unable to learn. Perceive any sequence of events that led up to this situation. Let the information flow surrounding this all-important future event now.

PLAY NEW AGE MUSIC FOR THREE MINUTES.

Sleep now and rest. You've done very well. Now, I want you to rise to the superconscious mind level to evaluate this future experience and apply this knowledge to your current life and situations. One, rising up; two, rising higher; three, halfway there; four, almost there; number five, you are there. Let your masters and guides assist you in making the most out of this experience. Do this now.

PLAY NEW AGE MUSIC FOR THREE MINUTES.

All right. Sleep now and rest. You did very, very well. Listen very carefully. I'm going to count backward now from five to one. This time, when I reach one, you will be back in the present, you will be able to remember everything you experienced and reexperienced, you'll feel very relaxed and refreshed and you'll be able to do whatever you have planned for the rest of the day or evening. You'll feel very positive about what you've just experienced, and very motivated about your confidence and ability to play this tape again to experience additional future events.

All right now. Five, moving back in time; four, moving farther back; three, halfway there; two, almost there; number one, you are back in the present. I'm going to count forward from one to five, and when I reach the count of five, you will be wide-awake, relaxed, and refreshed. Number one, very, very deep. Number two, you are getting a little bit lighter. Number three, halfway there. Number four, very, very light. Number five, awaken.

Angel Encounters

Angels are neither gods nor ghosts. These beings were created separately from humans and were given free will. Angels have consciousness and purpose. They may appear in dreams. Angels have no gender or corporeal (physical) body; they are pure spirit and were never a part of humankind. Angels exist because of human faith in them.

Angels do not interfere with free will; they merely offer advice and support. Motives must be pure for an angel contact to occur. This communication must be part of God's plan, and individuals must be prepared for such an encounter.

A Self-Hypnosis Exercise

To invite an encounter with an angel through hypnosis differs only slightly from a superconscious mind tap. Some minor differences may be noted in the following script.

Now listen very carefully. I want you to imagine a bright white light coming down from above and entering the top of your head, filling your entire body. See it, feel it, and it becomes reality. Now, imagine an aura of pure white light emanating from the region surrounding your heart, again surrounding your entire body, protecting you. See it, feel it, and it becomes reality. Now, only your angels and highly evolved, loving entities who mean you well will be able to influence you during this, or any other, hypnotic session. You are totally protected by this aura of pure white light.

In a few moments, I am going to count from one to 20. As I do so, you will feel yourself rising up to the superconscious mind level, from which you will be able to receive information from your angel protectors. Number one, rising up. Two, three, four, rising higher. Five, six, seven, letting information flow. Eight, nine, 10, you are halfway there. Eleven, 12, 13, feel yourself rising even higher. Fourteen, 15, 16, almost there. Seventeen, 18, 19, number 20, and you are there. Take a moment to orient yourself to the superconscious mind level.

PLAY NEW AGE MUSIC FOR ONE MINUTE.

You may contact any of your angels from this level. You may explore your relationship with any person. Remember, your superconscious mind level is all-knowing and has access to your akashic records (the memories of past, present, and future lives).

*Let your Higher Self send out the appropriate energy to attract one
of your angels.*

*Now, slowly and carefully state your desire for information
or an experience, and let this superconscious mind level work
for you.*

PLAY NEW AGE MUSIC FOR EIGHT MINUTES.

*You have done very well. Now I want you to further open up
the channels of communication by removing any obstacles and
allowing yourself to receive information and experiences that will
directly apply to, and help better, your present lifetime. Allow yourself to receive more advanced and more specific information from
your Higher Self and angels to raise your frequency and improve
your karmic subcycle. Do this now.*

PLAY NEW AGE MUSIC FOR EIGHT MINUTES.

*All right now. Sleep and rest. You did very well. Listen very
carefully. I'm going to count forward now from one to five. When
I reach the count of five, you will be back in the present; you will
be able to remember everything you experienced and reexperienced.
You'll feel very relaxed, refreshed, and you'll be able to do whatever you have planned for the rest of the day or evening. You'll feel
very positive about what you've just experienced, and very motivated about your confidence and ability to play this tape again to
experience your angels. All right now. One, very, very deep. Two,
you're getting a little bit lighter. Three, you're getting much, much
lighter. Four, very light. Five, awaken. Wide-awake and refreshed.*

Out-of-Body Experiences

Some people like to venture beyond their bodies to explore the universe and its multidimensional nature. This method provides evidence for
life after death, and is the mechanism for reincarnation.

A Self-Hypnosis Exercise

Try this exercise to experience an out-of-body experience for yourself.

Now, listen very carefully. I want you to imagine a bright white light coming down from above and entering the top of your head, filling your entire body. See it, feel it, and it becomes reality. Now, imagine an aura of pure white light emanating from the region surrounding your heart. Again, it surrounds your entire body, protecting you. See it, feel it, and it becomes reality. Now, only your masters and guides and highly evolved, loving entities who mean you well will be able to influence you during this, or any other, hypnotic session. You are totally protected by this aura of pure white light.

Now, as you focus in on how comfortable and relaxed you are, free of distractions, free from physical and emotional obstacles that prevent you from safely leaving and returning to the physical body, you will perceive and remember all that you encounter during this experience. When you are physically awake you will recall in detail only these matters that will be beneficial to your physical and mental being and experience. Now, begin to sense the vibrations around you and, in your own mind, begin to shape and pull them into a ring around your head. Do this for a few moments now.

PLAY NEW AGE MUSIC FOR TWO MINUTES.

Now, as you begin to attract these vibrations into your inner awareness, they begin to sweep throughout your body, making it rigid and immobile. You are always in complete control of this experience. Do this now, as you perceive yourself rigid and immobile, with these vibrations moving along and throughout your entire body.

PLAY NEW AGE MUSIC FOR THREE MINUTES.

You have done very well. Feel these vibrations. Perceive yourself feeling the pulse of these vibrations throughout your entire awareness. In your own mind's eye, reach out one of your arms and grasp some object that you know is out of normal reach. Feel the object and let your astral hand pass through it. Your mind is using your astral arm, not your physical arm, to feel the object. As you do this, you are becoming lighter and lighter, and your astral body is beginning to rise up from your physical body. Do this now.

PLAY NEW AGE MUSIC FOR THREE MINUTES.

You've done very well. Now, using other parts of your astral body (your head, feet, chest, and back), repeat this exercise and continue to feel lighter and lighter as your astral body begins to rise up from your physical body. Do this now.

PLAY NEW AGE MUSIC FOR THREE MINUTES.

Now, think of yourself as becoming lighter and lighter throughout your body. Perceive yourself floating up as your entire astral body lifts up and floats away from your physical body. Concentrate on blackness and remove all fears during this process. Imagine a helium-filled balloon rising and pulling your astral body with it, up and away from your physical body. Do this now.

PLAY NEW AGE MUSIC FOR THREE MINUTES.

Now, orient yourself to this new experience. You are out of your body, relaxed, safe, and totally protected by the white light. Concentrate on a place, not far away, that you would like to visit with your astral body. Now go to this place. Do this now. Perceive this new environment.

PLAY NEW AGE MUSIC FOR THREE MINUTES.

You've done very well. Now, I want you to travel to a destination much farther away. It can be a location across the country, or anywhere around the world. Take a few moments and think of this destination, and you will be there in a few moments. Do this now.

PLAY NEW AGE MUSIC FOR THREE MINUTES.

All right. Sleep now and rest. You did very, very well. Listen very carefully. I'm going to count forward now from one to five. When I reach the count of five, you will be back in your physical the body. You will be able to remember everything you experienced and reexperienced, you'll feel very relaxed refreshed, and you'll be able to do whatever you have planned for the rest of the day or evening. You'll feel very positive about what you've just experienced and very motivated about your confidence and ability to play this tape again to experience leaving your physical body safely. All right now. One, very very deep; two, you're getting a little bit lighter; three, you're getting much much lighter; four, very very light; five, awaken. Wide-awake and refreshed.

An Out-of-Body Experience Saves a Life

The main fear with regard to out-of-body experiences (OBEs) deals with its safety. In personally logging in more than 3,000 OBEs, and training thousands of patients to leave the body, I have never experienced or heard of any type of harm resulting from these techniques. Just the opposite occurs. As a result of these OBEs, I observe daily the fear of death eliminated, and physical, mental, emotional, and spiritual issues resolved. (To this I must add the many thousands of people who have experienced astral voyages using my audiotapes and subsequently informed me of their results.)

Consider the case of a recent college graduate, whom I shall call Tami. She came to my Los Angeles office in June 1996, from New York, to learn how to leave her body. I completed her training by the second week in June, and she then returned to New York.

Tami's plans were to travel to Europe and spend the last half of the summer there. She practiced the technique we worked on during her stay in Los Angeles, and became a fairly experienced subject by the month of July. At that time, she decided to fly to Paris to join some friends who wanted her to accompany them on their European trip. As a result of one of her OBEs, Tami saw that she was destined to die on her way to Paris.

Tami now had a problem. On the one hand, she was excited about going to Europe, but her OBEs had already demonstrated their accuracy in a few previous trips, during which she was able to see into the future and affect minor changes in her life. On the other hand, she feared that this trip would result in her death.

Tami decided not to depart for Europe until the end of July. Tami's original plans called for her leaving New York on July 17 on TWA flight 800. As you are well aware, this plane crashed shortly after leaving JFK International Airport, killing all 230 passengers and crew. Tami would have been victim 231 had she ignored her futuristic vision from her OBE.

Soul Plane Ascension

When a soul is in between lives, it travels to another dimension called the soul plane to select its next incarnation.

A soul plane ascension is actually an advanced superconscious mind tap. It is one of the most enlightening experiences that can be attained through hypnosis.

A Self-Hypnosis Exercise

The following script is one that I use in my office.

Now listen very carefully. I want you to imagine a bright white light coming down from above and entering the top of your head, filling your entire body. See it, feel it, and it becomes reality. Now, imagine an aura of pure white light emanating from the region surrounding your heart, again surrounding your entire body, protecting you. See it, feel it, and it becomes reality. Now, only your Higher Self and highly evolved loving entities who mean you well will be able to influence you during this, or any other, hypnotic session. You are totally protected by this aura of pure white light.

In a few moments, I am going to count from one to 20. As I do so, you will feel yourself rising up to the superconscious mind level, from which you will be able to receive information from your Higher Self. Number one, rising up. Two, three, four, rising higher. Five, six, seven, letting information flow. Eight, nine, 10, you are halfway there. Eleven, 12, 13, feel yourself rising even higher. Fourteen, 15, 16, almost there. Seventeen, 18, 19, number 20, you are there. Take a moment and orient yourself to the sub-conscious mind level.

PLAY ASCENSION MUSIC FOR ONE MINUTE.

Now, from the superconscious mind level, you are going to rise up and beyond the karmic cycle and the lower planes to the soul plane. The white light is always with you, and you may be assisted by your masters and guides as you ascend to the soul plane. Number one, rising up. Two, three, four, rising higher. Five, six, seven, letting information flow. Eight, nine, 10, you are half-way there. Eleven, 12, 13, feel yourself rising higher. Fourteen, 15, 16, almost there. Seventeen, 18, 19, number 20, you are there. Take a moment and orient yourself to the soul plane.

PLAY ASCENSION MUSIC FOR ONE MINUTE.

From the soul plane, you are able to perceive information from various sources and gain an overview of all your past lives, your current lifetime, and your future lives, including all your frequencies. Take a few moments now to evaluate this data and choose your next lifetime. Get a feel for the entire process.

PLAY ASCENSION MUSIC FOR SIX MINUTES.

You have done very well. Now, I want you to further open up the channels of communication by removing any obstacles and allowing yourself to receive information and experiences that will directly apply to and help better your present lifetime. Allow yourself to receive more advanced and more specific information from your Higher Self and guides to raise your frequency and improve your karmic subcycle here on Earth. Maintain the communication and connection with your Higher Self. You are one with your Higher Self. This connection will always exist, even when the physical body dies. Allow your Higher Self to instruct you. Do this now.

PLAY ASCENSION MUSIC FOR EIGHT MINUTES.

All right. Sleep now and rest. You did very, very well. Listen very carefully. I'm going to count forward now from one to five. When I reach the count of five, you will be back in your physical body. You will be able to remember everything you experienced and reexperienced; you'll feel very relaxed, refreshed; you'll be able to do whatever you have planned for the rest of the day or evening. You'll feel very positive about what you've just experienced and very motivated about your confidence and ability to enter into hypnosis again, to experience the soul plane. All right now. One, very, very deep. Two, you're getting a little bit lighter. Three, you're getting much, much lighter. Four, very, very light. Five, awaken. Wide-awake and refreshed.

Final Thoughts

In summary, the following statements with regard to consciousness may be made:

- Human beings are the aggregate of energy impulses. Each individual is connected to the energy of the universe.
- Energy and consciousness is what the human body, in essence, consists of. The physical body is a creation of the consciousness.
- Awareness through consciousness creates the biochemistry and anatomy of the body. It is the forgetting of true consciousness nature that results in difficulties by way of fears.
- Consciousness is always the primary aspect of being. Materialism is simply the creation of consciousness.

The following recommendations can be used to assist you in guiding your consciousness toward spiritual growth:

- Be at one with the infinite scheme of things. Practice hypnosis and meditation to attain this goal.
- Eliminate negative foods, drink, drugs, and toxic emotions from your life.
- Pay attention to your intuition and spiritual insights.
- Remember that everyone you meet, whether the meeting is a

positive or negative experience, is merely a projection of your consciousness. It is what you most dislike that you most deny in yourself. Use this to guide your spiritual growth.

◆ Eliminate the tendency to judge yourself and others.

◆ Do not seek external approval.

◆ Live life in the current moment and appreciate it fully. Let go of the past and do not worry about the future.

◆ Let go of all anger. When you do this, you will facilitate your own healing moderation of aging.

◆ Be motivated by love rather than fear.

Opening up your mind to all possibilities expands your levels of consciousness. Using self-hypnosis facilitates this openness and establishes the all-important connection with your Higher Self. Many spiritual-growth opportunities are available to the spiritually developed soul, but you must look for them. When you accept the concepts of a soul and a Higher Self, you enter a different universe, in which anything is possible and spiritual growth is the norm.

Conclusion

Self-hypnosis trains you to release the power that is within you. Hypnosis is as old as humankind, yet only a few have availed themselves of its benefits. Fear is the main reason why its use has not been maximized. Hypnosis represents a misunderstood power, and, invariably, humans fear anything that is powerful or that they don't understand. In ancient times, priests and kings exercised hypnosis as a divine power. They believed the gods had imparted to them a gift of power over their subjects.

These leaders were merely evoking a power that resides in everyone. This power, which resides within each of us and has caused us to see visions, hear the unheard, and accomplish the impossible, has been unleashed by hypnosis to make the sick well, the blind see, and the deaf hear. Hypnosis represents an innate power waiting to be used, governed, and controlled by each of us. Once properly instructed and conditioned, anyone can govern and control this force.

It is not yet understood why some people are more easily hypnotized than others, or why some go deeper into hypnosis than others. Furthermore, it is not yet understood exactly how hypnosis works, but it has been proved that it does.

The purpose of this book is to teach you how to use self-hypnosis intelligently so that you, too, can realize your full potential in life and permanently eliminate unwanted behavior. Self-hypnosis can make a positive contribution to every phase of your life—physically, mentally, and spiritually. Do not make the mistake of our ancestors by underestimating its power.

Using hypnosis to enhance life can be wonderful. Just from a suggestion, the mind can mold and create mental interpretations of sensations in ways that they had not been felt before. You can taste colors, smell textures, feel sounds, and enhance the strength of a sensation far greater than you have before. The time has come for hypnosis to come out of the closet. You must try something different in your quest for self-improvement. Hypnosis is not the only way to achieve this goal, it's just the most efficient.

The steps in using self-hypnosis can be summarized as:

1. Practice self-hypnotic induction techniques. Find one that is comfortable for you and use it daily.
2. Program your subconscious, by direct suggestions, to build up your self-image and confidence.
3. Use visual imagery, by way of mental movies, to establish goals and empower yourself.
4. Use post-hypnotic suggestions and program yourself to activate the subconscious appropriately whenever you are tempted to revert to previous dysfunctional behavior.
5. Program solutions to your trigger zones and use visualization techniques during your self-hypnosis to facilitate successful elimination of earlier negative responses.
6. Learn from your failures by treating them as new trigger zones, and use them to your advantage for continued improvement.
7. Keep using self-hypnosis after initial successes. Do not terminate this training and growth approach prior to achieving your goals.
8. Use cleansing to raise the quality of your subconscious mind's energy and permanently eliminate any self-defeating sequences.

In summarizing self-hypnosis, it can be stated that:

- You cannot be hypnotized against your will. And even after a hypnotic state is achieved, you will be able to hear, talk, think, act, or open your eyes at any time.
- Even a directly proposed hypnotic suggestion cannot make you do anything against your morals, religion, or self-preservation. If such a suggestion were given, you would either refuse to comply or would come out of the trance.
- The ego cannot be detached in hypnosis, so secrets will not come out while in trance, and you won't do anything you wouldn't typically do if you felt relaxed about the situation.
- The best hypnotic subjects are not unintelligent people. The more strong-willed, intelligent, and imaginative you are, the better subject you will probably be.

Most people who inquire about hypnosis are interested in one of the following: overcoming a problem; accomplishing an objective; or having an experience. Hypnosis is certainly no magic wand, but when used correctly it can give you an edge. It can provide you with a running start and help you to open all the necessary doors as you proceed toward achieving your goals.

Many wealthy, powerful, and famous people come to my Los Angeles office for hypnotherapy. You would think that with all of their fame, fortune, and influence these celebrities would be happy. They aren't, or else they would not be seeking help.

Motivation, discipline, and psychic empowerment are the most valuable qualities you can possess. Solving problems is easy once this is established. Self-hypnosis is the quickest and easiest road to your personal and professional growth.

Hypnosis is a proven and natural method for resolving problems quickly and easily. You can literally change your life and custom design your destiny using the simple exercises presented throughout this book.

As a society, we have become programmed to rely on drugs and health professionals to treat our issues. It is time for each of us to break these chains and become empowered. Try these simple time-tested techniques, and hypnotize your problems away.

NOTES

Chapter 1

1. H. Benson, *The Relaxation Response* (New York: William Morrow, 1975).
2. G.G. Scholem, *Jewish Mysticism* (New York: Schocken Books, 1967).
3. I. Veith, *Bulletin of Historical Medicine*, 37 (1963): 139.
4. F.J. MacHovec, "Hypnosis Before Mesmer," *American Journal of Clinical Hypnosis*, 17 (1973): 215.
5. M. Erickson, "An Experimental Investigation of the Possible Antisocial Uses of Hypnosis," Psychiatry, 2 (1939): 391–414.

Chapter 4

1. R.K. Wallace, et al., "Effects of the TM and TM-Sidhi program on the aging process," *International Journal of Neuroscience*, 16 (1982): 53–58.
2. C.N. Alexander, et al., "Transcendental Meditation, mindfulness and longevity: An experimental study with the elderly," *Journal of Personal Social Psychology*, 57 (1989): 950–964.
3. R. Greulich, N. Shock, et al., *Normal Human Aging* (Washington, D.C.: U.S. Government Printing Office, 1984).
4. J.K. Kiecolt-Glaser, et al., "Psychosocial Enhancement of Immuncompetence in a geriatric population." *Health Psychology* 4, 1985.

Chapter 5

1. T. Buzan, *Use Both Sides of Your Brain* (New York: E.P. Dutton, 1983).

Chapter 6

1. E. Roberts, L. Bologa, J.F. Flood, and G.E. Smith, "Effects of Dehydroepiandrosterone and Its Sulfate on Brain Tissue in Culture and on Memory in Mice," *Brain Research*, 406 (1987): 357–362.

2. B. Nasman, T. Olsson, T. Backstrom, S. Eriksson, K. Grankvist, M. Viitanen, and M. Bucht, "G. Serum dehydroepiandrosterone sulfate in Alzheimer's disease and in multiinfarct dementia," *Bio Psychiatry*, 30 (7) (1991): 684–690.

3. B. Nasman, et al.

4. M. Schrage, *Shared Minds: The New Technologies of Collaboration* (New York: Random House, 1990).

5. W. Harman and H. Rheingold, *High Creativity* (Los Angeles: J.P. Tarcher, 1984).

6. R.W. Clark, *Einstein: The Life and Times* (New York: World Publishing Co., 1974).

Chapter 8

1. C.T. Tart, "Stages of consciousness and state-specific sciences," *Science*, 176 (1972): 1203–1210.

2. W. Masters and V. Johnson, *Human Sexual Response* (Boston: Little, Brown and Co., 1966).

3. Ibid.

Chapter 10

1. S. Rosen, *The Reincarnation Controversy: Uncovering the Truth in the World Religions* (Badger, Calif.: Torchlight Pub., Inc., 1997).

RECOMMENDED READING

Abramson, E.E. *Behavioral Approaches to Weight Control*. New York: Springer Publishing Co., 1977.

Adams, J.L. *The Care and Feeding of Our Ideas: A Guide to Encouraging Creativity*. Reading, Mass.: Addison-Wesley Publishing Co., 1986.

Alexander, C.N., H.M. Chandler, E.J. Langer, R.I. Newman, and J.L. Davies, "Transcendental Meditation, Mindfulness and Longevity: An Experimental Study with the Elderly." *Journal of Personal Social Psychology* 57 (1989).

Behnke, J.A., C.E. Finch, and G.B. Moment, eds. *The Biology of Aging*. New York: Plenum Press, 1978.

Belliveau, F. and L. Richter. *Understanding Human Sexual Inadequacy*. Boston: Little, Brown and Co., 1970.

Benet, S. *How to Live to Be 100: The Life-Style of the People of the Caucasus*. New York: Dial Press, 1976.

Benson, H. *The Relaxation Response*. Boston: G.K. Hall, 1976.

Borysenko, J. *Minding the Body, Mending the Mind*. Reading, Mass.: Addison-Wesley Publishing Co., 1987.

Burnham, S. *A Book of Angels: Reflections on Angels Past & Present & True Stories of How They Touch Our Lives*. New York: Ballantine, 1990.

Butler, R.N. and M. Lewis. *Sex After Sixty: A Guide for Men and Women in Their Later Years*. New York: Harper & Row, 1976.

Buzan, T. *Use Both Sides of Your Brain*. New York: E.P. Dutton, 1983.

————. *Make the Most of Your Mind*. New York: Simon & Schuster, 1984.

Clark, R.W. *Einstein: The Life and Times*. New York: World Publishing Co., 1971.

Cooper, L. and M. Erickson. *Time Distortion in Hypnosis*. Baltimore: Williams & Wilkins, 1954.

Dunbar, F. *Mind and Body: Psychosomatic Medicine*. New York: Random House, 1955.

Erickson, M. "An Experimental Investigation of the Possible Antisocial Uses of Hypnosis." *Psychiatry*, 2 (1939): 391–414.

Fine, J. *Conquering Back Pain: A Comprehensive Guide*. New York: Prentice-Hall Press, 1987.

Fromm, E. "Altered States of Consciousness and Hypnosis: A Discussion." *International Journal of Clinical Experimental Hypnosis*, 25 (1977).

Gackenbach, J. and J. Bosveld. *Control Your Dreams*. New York: Harper & Row, 1989.

Gackenbach, J. and S. LaBerge. *Conscious Mind, Sleeping Brain*. New York: Plenum, 1988.

Goldberg, B. *Past Lives, Future Lives*. New York: Ballantine, 1988.

————. *Soul Healing*. St. Paul, Minn.: Llewellyn, 1996.

————. *Peaceful Transition: The Art of Conscious Dying and the Liberation of the Soul*. St. Paul, Minn.: Llewellyn, 1997.

————. *Look Younger, Live Longer: Add 25 to 50 Years to Your Life, Naturally*. St. Paul, Minn.: Llewellyn, 1998.

————. *Astral Voyages: Mastering the Art of Soul Travel*. St. Paul, Minn.: Llewellyn, 1999.

————. *Time Travelers from Our Future: A Fifth Dimension Odyssey*. Sun Lakes, Ariz.: Book World, Inc., 1999.

————. *Protected by the Light: The Complete Book of Psychic Self-Defense*. Tucson, Ariz.: Hats Off Books, 2000.

————. *New Age Hypnosis*. St. Paul, Minn.: Llewellyn, 1998.

————. *The Search for Grace: The True Story of Murder and Reincarnation.* St. Paul, Minn.: Llewellyn, 1997.

————. "Slowing Down the Aging Process through the Use of Altered States of Consciousness: A Review of the Medical Literature." *Psychology: A Journal of Human Behavior,* 32 (2), (1995): 19–22.

————. "Regression and Progression in Past Life Therapy." *National Guild of Hypnotists Newsletter,* 1, (Jan./Feb., 1994): 10.

————. "Quantum Physics and Its Application to Past Life Regression and Future Life Progression Hypnotherapy." *Journal of Regression Therapy,* 7(1), (1993): 89–93.

————. "Depression: A Past Life Cause." *National Guild of Hypnotists Newsletter* (Oct./Nov., 1993): 7, 14.

————. "The Clinical Use of Hypnotic Regression and Progression in Hypnotherapy." *Psychology: A Journal of Human Behavior,* 27 (1), (1990): 43–48.

————. "Your Problem May Come from Your Future: A Case Study."*Journal of Regression Therapy,* 4 (2), (1990): 21–29.

————. "The Treatment of Cancer through Hypnosis." *Psychology: A Journal of Human Behavior,* 3 (4), (1985): 36–39.

————. "Hypnosis and the Immune Response." *International Journal of Psychosomatics,* 32 (3), (1985): 34–36.

————. "Treating Dental Phobias through Past Life Therapy: A Case Report." *Journal of the Maryland State Dental Association,* 27 (3), (1984): 137–39.

Greulich, R.C., N. Schock, et al. *Normal Human Aging.* Washington, D.C.: U.S. Government Printing Office, 1984.

Harmon, W., and H. Rheingold. *Higher Creativity.* Los Angeles: J.P. Tarcher, 1984.

Head, J., and S.L. Cranston. *Reincarnation: The Phoenix Fire Mysteries.* New York: Julian, 1977.

Hodson, G. *Reincarnation: Fact or Fallacy.* Wheaton, Ill.: The Theosophical Publishing House, 1967.

Hutchinson, M.G. *Transforming Body Image: Learning to Love the Body You Have*. Freedom, CA: Crossing Press, 1985.

Jahn, R.G., and B. Dunne. *Margins of Reality: The Role of Consciousness in the Physical World*. New York: Harcourt, Brace, Jovanovich, 1987.

Karagulla, S. *Breakthrough to Creativity*. Santa Monica, CA: DeVross and Co., 1967.

Katz, J. "Psychophysiological Contributions to Phantom Limbs." *Canadian Journal of Psychiatry*, 37 (5), (1993): 282–298.

Kiecolt-Glaser, J.K., et al. "Psychosocial Enhancement of Immuncompetence in a Geriatric Population." *Health Psychology*, 4 (1985).

Korn, E.R. *Visualization: Use of Imagery in the Health Professions*. Homewood, Ill.: Dow-Jones-Irwin, 1983.

Langer, E. *Mindfullness*. Reading, Mass.: Addison-Wesley Publishing Co., 1989.

Loria, R.M., et al. "Immune Response Facilitation and Resistance to Virus and Bacterial Infections with Dehydroepiandrosterone (DHEA)." In *The Biologic Role of Dehydroepiandrosterone*, M. Kalimi, and W. Regelson, eds. New York: Walter de Gruyter, 1990.

MacHovec, F.J. "Hypnosis before Mesmer." *American Journal of Clinical Hypnosis*, 17 (1973): 215.

MacVaugh, G. *Frigidity: Successful Treatment in One Hypnotic Imprint Session with the Oriental Relaxation Technique*. New York: Medcon, Inc., 1972.

Maranto, G. "Aging: Can We Slow the Inevitable?" *Discover*, (Dec. 1984).

Masters, W., and V. Johnson. *Human Sexual Response*. Boston: Little, Brown and Co., 1966.

Melzak, R., and P.D. Wall. "Pain mechanisms: A new theory," *Science*, 150 (1965): 971–979.

Mills, J.C., and R.J. Crowley. *Therapeutic Metaphors for the Child Within*. New York: Brunner/Mazel, Inc., 1986.

Moore, J. *Sexuality and Spirituality: The Interplay of Masculine and Feminine in Human Development*. San Francisco: Harper-Collins, 1980.

Nasman, B., et al. "G-Serum Dehydroepiandrosterone Sulfate in Alzheimer's Disease and in Multi-infarct Dementia." *Biopsychiatry*, 30 (7), (1991): 684–690.

National Institute on Aging. *With the Passage of Time: The Baltimore Longitudinal Study of Aging, Pub. No. 93–3685*. Washington, D.C.: U.S. Government Printing Office, 1993.

———. *The Handbook for the Biology of Aging*. Washington, D.C.: U.S. Government Printing Office, 1985.

Penfield, W. *The Mystery of the Mind: A Critical Study of Consciousness and the Human Brain*. Princeton, N.J.: Princeton University Press, 1975.

Perry, C., and J.R. Laurence. "Hypnosis, Surgery, and Mind-body Interactions: A Historical Evaluation." *Canadian Journal of Behavioral Science*, 15 (1983): 351–372.

Philips, D., and R. Judd. *Sexual Confidence: Discovering the Joys of Intimacy*. Boston: Houghton Mifflin, 1980.

Regelson, W., et al. "Hormonal Intervention: 'Buffer Hormones' or 'State Dependency.' The Role of Dehydroepiandrosterone (DHEA), Thyroid Hormone, Estrogen and Hyphosectomy in Aging." *Annals of New York Academy of Science*, 521 (1988).

Richardson, A. *Mental Imagery*. New York: Springer Publishing Co., 1969.

Roberts, E., L. Bologa, and G.E. Smith. "Effects of Dehydroepiandrosterone and Its Sulfate on Brain Tissue in Culture and on Memory in Mice." *Brain Research*, 406 (1–2), (1987): 357–362.

Rosen, S. *The Reincarnation Controversy*. Badger, CA: Torchlight Pub. Inc., 1997.

Rosenberg, J. *Total Orgasm*. New York: Random House, 1976.

Scholem, G.G. *Jewish Mysticism*. New York: Schocken Books, 1967.

Schrage, M. *Shared Minds: The New Technologies of Collaboration*. New York: Random House, 1990.

Sommer, R. *The Mind's Eye: Imagery in Everyday Life*. New York: Delacorte Press, 1978.

Talbot, M. *The Holographic Universe*. New York: Harper Collins, 1991.

Tart, C. *Altered States of Consciousness*. New York: John Wiley & Sons, 1969.

———. "Stages of Consciousness and State-Specific Sciences." *Science*, 176 (1972): 1,203–1,210.

Wallace, R.K., M.C. Dillbeck, E. Jacobe, and B. Harrington. "Effects of the TM and TM-Sidhi Program on the Aging Process." *International Journal of Neuroscience*, 16 (1982).

Wolpe, J. *Psychotherapy by Reciprocal Inhibition*. Palo Alto, Calif.: Stanford University Press, 1958.

INDEX

ABOUT THE AUTHOR

Dr. Bruce Goldberg holds a B.A. degree in biology and chemistry, is a doctor of dental surgery, and has an M.S. degree in counseling psychology. He retired from dentistry in 1989 and has concentrated on his hypnotherapy practice in Los Angeles. In 1975, Dr. Goldberg was trained by the American Society of Clinical Hypnosis in the techniques and clinical applications of hypnosis.

Dr. Goldberg has been interviewed on shows such as *Sally, Donahue, Oprah, Leeza, Joan Rivers, The Other Side, Regis and Kathie Lee, Tom Snyder, Jerry Springer, Jenny Jones*, and *Montel Williams* as well as by CNN, CBS news, and many other programs. Through lectures, television and radio appearances, and magazine and newspaper articles, including interviews in *Time*, the *Los Angeles Times*, and the *Washington Post*, he has conducted more than 35,000 past-life regressions and future-life progressions since 1974, helping thousands of patients empower themselves through these techniques. His cassette tapes teach people self-hypnosis and guide them into past and future lives and time travel. He gives lectures and seminars on hypnosis, regression and progression therapy, time travel, and conscious dying; he is also a consultant to corporations, attorneys, and the local and network media.

His first edition of *The Search for Grace* was made into a television movie by CBS. His third book, the award-winning *Soul Healing*, is a classic on alternative medicine and psychic empowerment. *Past Lives-Future Lives* is Dr. Goldberg's international bestseller and is the first book written on future lives (progression therapy).

For information on self-hypnosis tapes, speaking engagements, or private sessions, Dr. Goldberg can be contacted directly by writing to:

Bruce Goldberg, D.D.S., M.S.

4300 Natoma Avenue

Woodland Hills, CA 91364

Telephone: (800) KARMA-4-U or (800) 527-6248

Fax: (818) 704-9189

email: drbg@sbcglobal.net

Web Site: *www.drbrucegoldberg.com*

Please include a self-addressed, stamped envelope with your letter.

OTHER BOOKS BY
BRUCE GOLDBERG

Past Lives-Future Lives

Soul Healing

The Search for Grace:
A Documented Case of Murder and Reincarnation

Peaceful Transition:
The Art of Conscious Dying and the Liberation of the Soul

New Age Hypnosis

Secrets of Self-Hypnosis

Unleash Your Psychic Powers

Look Younger and Live Longer:
Add 25 to 50 Quality Years to Your Life, Naturally

Protected by the Light:
The Complete Book of Psychic Self-Defense

Time Travelers from Our Future:
A Fifth Dimension Odyssey

Astral Voyages:
Mastering the Art of Soul Travel

Custom Design Your Own Destiny

Self-Hypnosis

Karmic Capitalism: A Spiritual Approach to Financial Independence

CPSIA information can be obtained
at www.ICGtesting.com
Printed in the USA
LVHW051541050522
718029LV00002B/350